Praise for *Engagement from Scratch!*

"Pragmatic, appealing, pleasurable to read. Engagement from Scratch is a "must" for anyone who wants to build a business in this era of the social Internet."

David Garfinkel, top copywriter, Author of Guerrilla Copywriting and many other books, and co-founder of FastEffectiveCopy.com

"Engagement From Scratch will show you exactly what you need to know to build something bigger than yourself. A business. A community. A movement. I had multiple light bulbs go off within the first ten pages. This book is good. Very good. Choose to ignore the principles in this book and business will be much harder."

James Clear, Passive Panda

"It use to be that only marketers and rockstars had to worry about audience, but now every business and blogger needs to have one. Engagement from Scratch covers the skills that everyone should know about building an audience, whether for a company or for themselves, as explained by the people who have been there and done it."

Adam Berke, President of AdRoll.com

"Danny has captured the essence of what really works from a virtual who's who of super community builders. Every business, blogger, and community manager desiring to effectively grow their online influence can directly apply the wisdom found in this book."

Gail Gardner, Social Media Marketing and Internet Strategist, GrowMap.com

"Finally! Danny wrote a game-changing book about one of today's most important business building tools. Run, don't walk, to grab your copy!"

Julie Steelman, Author of The Effortless Yes!, www.JulieSteelman.com

"When I see a book that has over a dozen of contributors, skepticism is one of my first reactions. In fact, this is quite possibly the feeling that most of us have about books with multiple authors... unless, of course, they are encyclopedias or compilations of highly-targeted articles on niche topics. When putting together a book like this, there are always two risks: either running it all too shallow, or aggregating a volume of articles which, while being individually interesting, may not read well together.

"Engagement from Scratch is a notable exception. Danny Iny has done an amazing job of making articles of some thirty experts flow like a well-orchestrated musical composition. This book is a must-read for every modern-day entrepreneur. In it you'll find practical, advice on how to grab people's attention, cultivate loyalty, and build what we're all ultimately after -- the ongoing engagement. Grab it before your competition does! It is an easy, yet an important read on the topic."

Evgenii "Geno" Prussakov, Speaker, digital marketing consultant, author of Affiliate Program Management: An Hour a Day

"After glancing over the cover for the book, I knew instantly this book was full of rock-solid information from the many blogger personalities I read already. Couldn't wait to dive in and read it. Danny certainly delivered as promised. The stories are insightful how each person engages audiences differently from the next, but the point may surprise you...

"Even if you're in business to make money, you're touching each and every person with a part of you. And not only that, but the people around you connect with each other. If you truly want a memorable, engaging experience for your blog, the contributors in Danny's book use their stories to show you how to do it. I took away so many tips and insight to use as inspiration to continue growing my blog."

Gabrielle Conde, Mission Engage

"Danny Iny has created a forum for some dynamic thinkers to share their insights in the process of establishing yourself in that space. To be expected, some will resonate with you, and some won't. But, more than any specific tips and tricks, is the wide range of ideas here and the simple humanity required for "success". It is a testament to Danny that he could get so many to summon that into one book."

Matthew Stillman, StillmanSays.com

"The really cool thing about 'Engagement from Scratch' is that Danny puts me face-to-face with each of these leaders. Each chapter is a warm, by-the-fireplace experience written by someone who honestly cares about his or her community. And when I read the book, I felt like I was getting an intimate, 1-on-1 experience. This book is required for anyone hoping to give more than he takes, build more than he destroys, and produce more than he consumes."

Craig A Gonzales, Craig Gonzales Tutoring

"Since providing content is my bread and getting people to engage is my butter, I'd like to think I already know a fair bit about the principles of engagement, how to build community, and how to be passionate. But I was wrong. I read every word of this book, without having to fight my inner-skimmer, and I took pages of notes about best practices and ideas that will catapult my business forward.

"The contributors made this book about engagement one that is truly engaging. They are masters of their craft and I appreciate Danny having them sound off in one great book."

Peggy Baron, PeggyBaron.com

"What's interesting about this particular publication is that the individual stories of all the contributing authors tie together and create one actionable and inspirational resource. When you see a book by one single author then there's only one approach that they give to the reader - the "good approach that has worked for me - the author".

"But here, the situation is different. Different people, with different stories, so in the end you can see that each person has a unique approach to success (and all of them good), and in the end it's for you to decide what path you want to take yourself, or how to combine different advice from different people into your own plan."

Karol K, online business designer and blogger, newInternetOrder.com

"Engagement from Scratch! hits the mark!!! I came away with not one, not several, but MANY tips. This book is about more than just engaging, it is about caring, connecting & building. Caring about your readers, connecting in your relationships and building your audience as a community."

Meo Cuenca, Progressive Mommy Blogger at Merciful Blessings

"Practical and easy to read, it offers a real opportunity to learn from the experts in building a tribe. This is a book you'll come back to again and again."

Claire Kerslake

"Whether you're new to blogging, have a small community of subscribers, or already have an established active audience, this book will help you identify ways to keep your audience engaged within your community. It's undeniably a blueprint full of strategies to cross-reference and implement to mark your place in the crowded blogosphere. As a blogger I found the insights of the successful community-builders not only helpful, but practical. The versatility of the perspectives shared in this book is what makes this such an interesting read. How inspiring is it to read about the steps used by the high-profile bloggers whose content we take for granted every day?! They provide real strategies and tactics to implement as you work to build your own community. You will highlight sections and make notes in the margins like I did!

"I can't wait to get a copy of this book. I feel like I can actually build my own dynamic community. I'm new to blogging and I had not considered the possibility of my blog evolving into a community. Now it seems quite possible!"

Kemya Scott, Phisco Marketing

"I really enjoyed reading through the contributions of the different authors - they're very well organized, and contain a lot of useful information that I am planning on putting into practice!"

Tracy Collins, Commission Maniac Blog (tlkool9.blogspot.com)

"This book is the gold nugget, the missing link for online marketing for small business. I have done many courses and read many books, spending thousands of dollars and hundreds of hours trying to discover how to market online for my small business. Finally Danny has provided the answer. He has gone to the best experts for you, got the answers, and then made them cheaply and succinctly available to you. If you can read only one book this year, read this one!"

Virginia Graham, Model Mortgages (.com.au)

ENGAGEMENT

from scratch!

HOW SUPER-COMMUNITY BUILDERS
CREATE A LOYAL AUDIENCE
AND HOW YOU CAN DO THE SAME!

Do You Need Help Building Your Own Engaged Audience?

This book contains the most important lessons learned by some of the world's most successful audience- and community-builders about how they built an engaged and loyal audience, and how they would do it all again.

To help you put their advice into practice, we've created a whole goodie bag of extra stuff for you:

- ✓ Detailed infographics clearly laying out the entire process taught in the book
- ✓ Worksheets to help you do everything that is discussed in the book, and do it well
- ✓ Templates that you can use to approach bloggers and build relationships
- ✓ Access to exclusive teleseminars, webinars, and coaching calls
- ✓ And a whole bunch of other cool stuff...

Does that sound awesome or what? Go get it now:

bit.ly/efs-bonus

ENGAGEMENT
from scratch!

HOW SUPER-COMMUNITY BUILDERS
CREATE A LOYAL AUDIENCE
AND HOW YOU CAN DO THE SAME!

Danny Iny

CO-FOUNDER OF FIREPOLE MARKETING

This book is dedicated to Bhoomi.

Sweetie, you are my wife, better half, and best friend; you make me feel blessed every morning and every night.

Table of Contents

Foreword by C.C. Chapman

I grew up in a small town in New Hampshire, in what is lovingly known as "The Upper Valley". It was the kind of place where kids would ride their bikes to get wherever they were going, and you knew the people behind the shop counters by their first names.

Even if you hadn't met someone before, you could be sure that someone you knew had, and they'd openly tell you their opinion of them. Good or bad, you couldn't escape the reputation that followed you.

Today, no matter where you live in the world, you also live in the small town of the Internet. Sure, it's global and growing every single second, but at its heart it operates very much like the small town in which I grew up.

Building a community is not rocket science, and it isn't something that you can force, buy, or magically make happen faster than it naturally wants to. Many have tried, and many more have failed. As you'll read in the forthcoming pages, it takes time, work and compassion to get there.

You'll hear from many unique voices in this book as they share their success stories. As you'll find, there are some overarching themes that each of them contain, and as you prepare to read them, that is what I want you to focus on.

Passion must be in your heart and at the top of your mind every morning when you get up and prepare to push forward. I'm a firm believer that passion is contagious, and if yours is genuine, people will be attracted to it. You have to be the perfect mix of cheerleader, scout master and army general in order to build and foster your community.

If you are creating something that you are passionate about people will find it and be attracted. Don't be constantly selling and shilling. Figure out how you can help others, tell them stories, and share openly everything you know so that people will recognize you as someone that they can trust, who won't turn them off by constantly trying to sell them something.

People want to connect with people that they aspire to be like, and who they can at the same time approach directly and without hesitation. The most successful of us have figured out how to achieve that balance as our network of friends, connections and followers have grown.

Be yourself, and be human. I've watched too many budding entrepreneurs think that the only thing they can ever talk about and share is their company. While this should always be top of mind, the successful ones among us are the ones who share all sides of themselves. The ones who share more about their lives are the ones who allow more to connect.

In my book, *Content Rules*, we talk about the concept of a campfire, and how every day you must be thinking about what you can add to the fire that will keep people coming back by burning ever higher. They need to feel welcomed and amazed at the same time.

As you add to this fire, the people will go out and tell those stories to others. They'll start conversations with "I've got to tell you..." and "Did you hear about..." and then will share their experience interacting with you. You can talk about yourself over and over, what you really want is others to do the talking for you. That is how your community will grow.

Getting to the people who already know you, trust you and are excited by you is easy. The trick is to get *them* talking about you, and inspiring them to the point that they *can't not* talk about you to their friends and followers. Never stop nurturing your immediate network, but always try to reach out and bring in their extended network as well.

The best piece of business advice I was ever given was to find a mentor who would challenge you.

In the following pages you'll meet a slew of great mentors who will open up, share their best advice, and challenge you to be better. The best thing about most of them is that because they understand the small town mentality, if you contact them after reading what they had to say, I bet they'll respond because they are building their own community, and know that *every single person matters*.

Always remember that if you are good to others and never stop working hard, amazing things will happen. I wish you the best of luck on your entrepreneurial journey, and hope our paths cross at some point.

C.C. Chapman
Founder of *DigitalDads.com*
Co-Author of *Content Rules*

ENGAGEMENT FROM SCRATCH!

Introduction

Have you ever marveled at the fanatically engaged communities surrounding the Guy Kawasakis and Brian Clarks of the world? Seen and felt how intensely connected and loyal the audience was to the work and ideas of the person that they followed?

And have you wondered how you can create an equally engaged audience for your own blog, business, or cause?

If you have, then you and I share something in common: We've both wondered what creates that sort of connection – what secret ingredients foster that kind of intense loyalty, and what recipe can be followed to find and attract those loyal followers to your cause?

I wrote *Engagement from Scratch!* for both of us. And really, "wrote" is the wrong word – "assembled" better describes my role in this project. You see, over the last year, as I built my own following at Firepole Marketing, I've learned some of the answers to those questions – and realized that there are so many more questions that I need the answers to.

So I reached out to the people who did have the answers, and asked them the one question that had been on my mind for so long, and is probably on your mind as well: "If you had to start over and build an engaged audience from scratch, how would you do it?"

This book contains their answers to that question. Their answers were very varied in nature. Some spoke about mindset, and others spoke about tactics. Some told me what I expected to hear, and others surprised me with ideas I hadn't considered. Some came in the form of a thoughtful, reflective exercise, and some came in the form of a step-by-step set of instructions.

Looking at all the answers, I realized that there is no one answer to the question – there are many paths up the mountain, and what we need isn't a roadmap, but rather a compass that we can use to find our own way.

It is my hope that the answers contained in this book will serve as that compass for you.

Can You Help Me?

I created this book because I saw bloggers and entrepreneurs dying to know how they could create an audience from scratch, and I wanted to provide them with an answer.

I'm not in it for the money – I'm giving away the digital version of the book for free, and half of the profits from hard-copy sales are going to the Network for Teaching Entrepreneurship. I just want to get this content out to the people who need it.

I'm not a big publishing company, and I don't have a big marketing budget, ties to the media, or relationships with booksellers.

The only thing that I've got going for me is you, my reader. So I'm asking for a small favor: can you help me spread the word?

You could tell your friends and loved ones about this book, or even buy them a copy. Or you could visit the site, and use the buttons on the homepage to tweet, like and share the book to your networks. You could even go to Amazon.com, and write a review.

I know that I can count on you. Thank you in advance for your help, and for being a part of my own engaged audience.

www.EngagementFromScratch.com

My Story of Engagement from Scratch

For me, "scratch" was less than a year ago.

Sure, I had some things going for me, but as far as an audience goes, it was zilch. Nada. Bubkus.

My partner and I had just launched a promising new venture called Firepole Marketing, that offered a marketing training program for small businesses, entrepreneurs, and non-marketers.

We had already built the training program, and had just launched our brand new blog. We had no readers, no subscribers, and no relationships with big players in the industry.

Fast forward less than a year, and Firepole Marketing has become a household name in my corner of the marketing world. Hundreds of thousands of people have read my work, our training program is full of students… and I just co-authored the book that you're reading now with Guy Kawasaki, Brian Clark, Mitch Joel, and all of the other wonderful superstars whose ideas and experiences are shared in the following pages.

So… how did I get from there to here?

What was scratch, exactly?

Let's start by getting a sense of where I was at when all of this started.

I had founded a start-up company in 2007, which had crashed and burned by the end of 2008, a victim of the economic crash and my lack of experience as a CEO (this was my first big start-up, and I was only 25 years old at the time). I found myself with a quarter million dollars of debt, struggling to fill a pipeline of consulting clients.

So I hustled.

I reached out to all of my past clients, and went to every networking event that I could find. I rebuilt my consulting practice, started paying off my debt, and got back on my feet.

Along the way, I met Peter Vogopoulos on the networking circuit, and we quickly hit it off. Peter was (and is) a business and marketing coach, serving the same type of client that I do: entrepreneurs and small businesses in the 0-10 employee range.

We had both noticed that there were a lot of people in our target market who really needed help, but had little or no money to pay for it. Not everybody, of course – there were plenty of businesses that were doing very well, and there were more than enough of them to support a thriving consulting and coaching practice for Peter and myself. But there were a lot of people who really needed help.

And we wanted to help. We both gave away a lot of our time for free, but we couldn't keep up with the demand – free advice just couldn't scale.

We looked for some sort of training solution that we could refer them to, but we couldn't find anything suitable on the market. Everything we found was either too complex, or too convoluted, or too tactical – there was nothing out there that would teach people how to market their business and get real results.

We realized that if we wanted a solution to offer these entrepreneurs and business owners, we would have to build it ourselves – and that's exactly what we did. Why did we think we could build a better program? Well, we had something special going for us. Sure, we were both skilled marketers, but we were also experienced educators – me thanks to my educational technology start-up experience, and Peter by virtue of being a popular faculty member at the John Molson School of Business at Concordia University.

So we put our heads together, and built the training program that became the flagship product of Firepole Marketing. Towards the end of 2010, the training program was nearing completion, and our blog went live at FirepoleMarketing.com.

It was time to start building our audience.

Failed First Attempt: A Lesson in Viral Marketing

They say that the shoemaker goes barefoot, and that certainly applied in our case – as skilled as we were at marketing, somehow it's always easier to apply your skills and expertise to other people's businesses than to your own.

We started the year with a contest on the blog, in which entrants could win over $10,000 in marketing and branding services. We ran seven posts about our FIRE-PROOF Selling System, and there was a question at the end of each post. To enter the contest, people had to share the posts with their networks, and leave a comment answering each question. Simple enough, right?

Then we had our big launch – three videos, a bunch of emails to our list, the whole shebang.

So what were the sales results? Nada – we didn't sell a thing.

In hindsight, this isn't surprising. Prior to the contest, we were getting about ten readers per day – on a good day. We got a small influx of traffic from a guest post on Copyblogger, but the numbers were still pretty low. There is a formula for virality, with a few essential elements that we had ignored. Here's the formula:

$$VIRALITY = EPIC\ SHIT^2 \cdot \sqrt{CRITICAL\ MASS} \cdot ACTION \left(\frac{reach}{friction}\right)$$

EPIC SHIT: In the words of Corbett Barr, who coined the phrase *Write Epic Shit*: "Write things that make people think. Inspire people. Change lives. Create value. Blow people away with your usefulness." This is critical. It doesn't matter what else you do, if your content isn't impossibly awesome, it will *never* go viral. Create content that you would expect people to pay for, then give it away for free. Epic shit has exponential impact.

CRITICAL MASS: We've all heard the standard line about virality – you show something to three people, each of them shows it to another three people, each of them shows it to three people, and pretty soon your server crashes from the massive increase in traffic. That's what we were depending on with our contest. Well, in real life, if you show it to three people, one won't look, one will read it and do nothing

11

and the third might tell three friends, but those three friends probably won't listen. You need to have a certain amount of attention for there to be a critical mass that can send your content sailing over the tipping point.

ACTION: The third element is action. For something to go viral, it isn't enough for people to like and read it, they must also share it (sharing is action) Sometimes, people will spontaneously share something past that tipping point, but it usually happens on sites like Facebook, YouTube, or Twitter, where the reach of that sharing action is huge, and the friction in taking that sharing action is tiny (you just click a "like" button).

These three factors make a recipe: start with truly epic content, plan the different sources of traffic that will feed it (guest posts are great for this, so is reaching out to your network for help), then make sure to include a way for people to share easily and reach a lot of people. We didn't have all the ingredients; critical mass, in particular, was missing.

At the end of the launch, our baseline of 5-10 visitors per day had gone up to about 25-35 – an increase off about 300%, which is great, but nowhere near the numbers that we needed to achieve our goals.

Why Guru Strategies DON'T Work

Every soldier knows that when things don't go the way you had hoped and planned, you fall back on your training.

That's exactly what we did. We took a step back, pretended we were consulting for a client, and put on our expert marketer hats. We took stock of our situation, and asked the exact same questions that we would ask a client if they approached us for help with this exact problem.

Suddenly, it didn't seem complicated at all. We were expecting the results that you would get with an audience that filled a stadium, but our audience could squeeze into a large living room.

Remember the phrase, "to everything there is a season"? The one that the Byrds copied from the book of Ecclesiastes (but everyone thinks it was the Beatles)?

The same thing applies to growing a blog (or anything, for that matter). Start at the beginning, then work your way up one step at a time. Knockout strategies *can* work, but they require a solid scaffolding that a blog with minimal traffic just doesn't have.

Try to run before you learn to walk, and you'll never stop crawling.

One of the best explanations for this phenomenon comes from Dan Dennett, who introduced the concept of "skyhooks and cranes" in his book "Darwin's Dangerous Idea" (he uses it to explain evolution by natural selection, but his metaphor applies perfectly to blogging).

Let's say that you want to build a skyscraper. In a perfect, imaginary world, you'd use a skyhook – a large hook in the sky to which you could attach a pulley system to raise objects from the ground. But skyhooks don't exist. It's impossible to make a hook float in the air.

From Wikipedia: "...the term "skyhook" describe[s] a source of design complexity that does not build on lower, simpler layers – In simple terms, a miracle."

That's the flimsy promise that most bombastic Internet marketing products are built on: massive growth on a foundation of feathers. In simple terms, a miracle.

So skyhooks are out – does that mean we can't build anything?

Of course we not. But to build our wondrous concrete jungles, we must use cranes.

Cranes serve the same purpose as skyhooks, only we build them from the ground up. Here's the fascinating part: the way to build a giant crane with tons of leverage is to *use smaller cranes!*

Build something massive by starting with something small to effectively close the distance.

The point isn't that you should be patient, taking things slow and steady with the belief that you'll eventually finish the race. No, the point is that the fastest way to get big is *by using the strategy that naturally fits with your current stage of growth*. The more your strategy is tailored to your current stage of growth, the faster you'll outgrow it and be ready for the next one!

There are four distinct stages involved in growing an audience online, that every blog and website has to go through:

Stage 1: Truly Awesome Content – Know who your audience is, and create something extraordinary for them.

Stage 2: Build Your Community – Connect with your other people who can help you along the way – not just the big players that you look up to, but also your peers, who are trying to do the same thing that you are.

Stage 3: Be Everywhere – Do the work to become ubiquitous in the eyes of your audience (more on this in a moment).

Stage 4: Get Viral – Harness the formula that I outlined earlier to generate some real virality and growth, but only when you've got the critical mass for it to work.

We tried to jump straight from stage 1 to stage 4 – no wonder it didn't work!

I first outlined this framework in my post about "Why Guru Strategies for Blog Growth DON'T WORK… and What Does!", which ironically went viral, garnering almost 200 comments at last count, and ratcheting up the size of our audience. The framework eventually formed the skeleton of a book that I co-authored with Sean Platt, called **"How to Build a Blog: Create Awesome Content, Build Community, and Go Viral!"** (Look it up on Amazon!)

So I followed my own framework.

I built relationships with other bloggers in my community – not just the people that I look up to (many of whom ended up contributing to this book), but also many of my peers, whose blogs were as small as mine, or smaller. I read their posts, left comments when I had something to say, and often took the relationship "offline", corresponding via email or over the phone.

Then it was time to "be everywhere".

This is the part of the story where Firepole Marketing really grew into a household name online, and I started being touted as a blogger and marketer to watch. It seemed to a lot of people as though I was everywhere (in the words of Eugene Farber, who coined the phrase, *"Wow, Danny, you're like the Freddy Krueger of blogging – wherever I turn, you're there!"*).

But I wasn't really everywhere…

The Freddy Krueger of Blogging

It started innocently enough.

I was in Jon Morrow's guest blogging program, and received the latest lesson in my inbox, explaining that list posts were the easiest way to break into a big blog, because they usually performed well and were exhausting to produce.

As luck would have it, I had just developed a curriculum of business books for a client. So I emailed Jon and asked him if he thought it would be a good fit for Copyblogger. Jon said that he couldn't make any promises, but that I should send him a draft, so I worked my tail off to write a stellar post, and Copyblogger ran it.

The post performed well; 200+ comments, 900+ tweets, and tons of traffic back to Firepole Marketing. I even got an email from Guy Kawasaki (I had mentioned one of his books on the list) that eventually turned into an interview, book reviews, and Guy's excellent contribution to the book that you're reading today.

I figured that since Copyblogger had worked so well, I'd try my hand at another guest post, and emailed Problogger to see if they wanted to publish the story of my experience.

It was a total shot in the dark, and there wasn't any kind of "in" – just a cold email through the contact form. It was a long shot, but it never hurts to try. To my great (and pleasant) surprise, they went for it. The result was my first post on Problogger. This led to more notoriety, and more traffic back to Firepole Marketing.

I realized that guest blogging was a great idea, and that I needed to do more of it. But where? And how? I felt that I'd been lucky with Copyblogger and Problogger. What now? Who would take my posts? Who would even answer my emails?

I did some research, and made a list of blogs that I wanted to guest post on. (Interesting note: even though my first guest post was on Copyblogger, I was so intimidated by their size and quality that it took another 14 guest posts before I worked up the courage to pitch them again.)

I emailed about a dozen bloggers, figuring that I would probably only hear back from a fraction of them, and most of the responses would be rejections. At best, I was hoping to end up with one guest post, maybe two.

Except that it turns out that bloggers are a lot easier to reach than I thought they would be, and if you do your homework and make a solid, concise pitch, they're likely to respond in your favor. And they did – all of them

My first thought: "Great!"

My second thought: "Oh, crap, now I have to write a dozen posts, and I have to do it all in the next week or two!"

I was under the gun. This was a great opportunity, but if I blew it, or showed them that I wasn't reliable, I probably wouldn't get another chance.

So I buckled down and wrote.

And wrote.

And wrote.

And wrote some more.

Then the posts all started to go live.

Having all these guest posts run within a few weeks of each other was a happy accident, but I learned something very important from the experience: *The value of guest posts increases exponentially with the number of concurrent posts that you write.*

In other words, two simultaneous guest posts is worth a lot more than two individual posts, three are worth a LOT more than two, and so forth.

This returns to the truism we've all learned about the number of impressions you need to make in order for people to notice you, plus with people's tendency to forget, and get distracted.

Imagine a "meter of attention." Every time people see you, that meter inches higher. But then, whenever they aren't seeing you, it slowly dips back down. Space your appearances out over a large period of time, and you lose much of the effect.

Do them at the same time, and you'll see two benefits. Not only will you avoid losing momentum between posts, but people will also start talking about you, leading to even more attention and awareness. All of that comes together to move you past the threshold of "getting noticed", and after that, it gets easier. You need less of an introduction because people already know who you are.

Once I realized what was happening, I could make it intentional – as I did when we did a big launch before closing our training program to the public at the end of August 2011.

Looking at the Big Picture

That launch was a watershed moment for Firepole Marketing, and for me.

Several months earlier, after having begun to ride the waves of growth that we were experiencing, I spent a weekend looking at the big picture, planning where I wanted to go next with my audience, and my life.

On the personal side, I knew exactly where I was going – I was engaged to the most wonderful woman that I've ever met, and we were getting married in early September.

On the business side, I wanted to make sure that we weren't just growing an audience for the sake of growing an audience, and that what we were building would ultimately support the lifestyle that I wanted to create, and do it in accordance with the values that we wanted to serve.

That weekend of reflection was the start of the book that you're reading now.

You see, when I set out to build an audience, it was because we needed a way of marketing our training program – that's all. But along the way, I spent hundreds of hours interacting with other people who had built audiences. I read their posts, commented on their work, corresponded with them via email, and spoke with them on the phone. I came to respect and admire many of them, and in some cases, what started as a professional connection has become a true friendship.

And therein lies the most important lesson that I learned while building my audience: that an audience is more than just the sum of the strategies and tactics that brought its constituent members together. A loyal and strong audience is much more than just a bunch of readers – it is a living and breathing entity that ties real people together.

In other words, it's a community.

Have you got the FREE audience-building goodie bag?

You didn't buy or download this book for fun – you did it because you care about building an engaged audience, just like the co-authors of the book have done, and would do again.

Well, we want to help, so we've created a whole goodie bag of extra stuff for you:

- ✓ Detailed infographics clearly laying out the entire process taught in the book
- ✓ Worksheets to help you do everything that is discussed in the book, and do it well
- ✓ Templates that you can use to approach bloggers and build relationships
- ✓ Access to exclusive teleseminars, webinars, and coaching calls
- ✓ And a whole bunch of other cool stuff...

Does that sound awesome or what? Go get it now:

bit.ly/efs-bonus

Section 1: General Principles

The first section of the book is about general principles of audience building – what you need to understand in terms of strategy and mindset in order to get started.

Alexander Osterwalder's article, "The Audience and the Business Model", shares his view that new and innovative ideas can work, as long as you're meeting real audience needs.

Brian Clark's essay, "Build the Audience, and Opportunity Will Come", tells you that if you listen, your audience will tell you what to create.

Danny Brown's article, "Build Your Goals First", goes into why you must have a laser-focused understanding of who your audience is, and what you want from them.

Guy Kawasaki's contribution, "99 Happy People", explains that the road to an engaged audience is paved with the three pillars of enchantment: likeability, trustworthiness, and quality.

Mark W. Schaefer's essay, "Community through Tenacity", tells you why building a great community is just the beginning.

Mitch Joel's essay, "Be Damn Interesting", teaches that your audience doesn't have to be your client base, but your client base must be part of your audience.

Randy Komisar's article, "An Unlikely Audience", shares his view that authenticity is everything.

Stuart Mills's contribution, "There Is No Set Path", explains that there is no "one-size-fits-all" way to build an audience.

Without further ado, let's get to it… the general principles of growing an engaged audience, from scratch.

Alexander Osterwalder: The Audience and the Business Model

New and innovative ideas can work as long as you're meeting real audience needs.

Growing an audience takes time, and can be approached from many different angles.

I first started creating an audience when I was completing my PHD in the study of Business Models. I put my doctoral dissertation online, and people started downloading it. Eventually, I began blogging about the concepts that I researched, and Wikipedia sourced it as a definition of "Business Models".

I'm not suggesting that you go out and get a PHD in your niche – I'm just telling you this as an example of the different ways in which an online presence can be developed. Mine grew around the research that I had done as a doctoral candidate.

In the beginning, most of my traffic came from that Wikipedia reference, and I supported that by blogging with a "freemium" mindset; I shared my thoughts, knowledge and research with people through my blog and the other interesting new technologies I had access to, such as Twitter and Facebook. Another platform that I got a lot of mileage out of was SlideShare. I put my most of the slides of my talks and presentations on their website, and even made some presentations specifically for SlideShare – tailored to go viral. People could go through them at their leisure.

People told me that I was crazy to be giving away so much information for free, but if I hadn't followed the freemium model, and shared my content freely, I wouldn't be where I am today, with the audience that I currently have. As I started becoming more of a recognized authority on the subject, invitations to speak followed.

One thing that was hugely important to me through this process was to remain focused on my expertise. My interest is in business models, so that's what I shared information about. Certainly it's a broad area, but there is always a temptation to stray off topic. Focusing allows you to have an audience who knows what to expect when they come to you. It's a promise you're able to keep consistently, and it enhances your credibility.

The Book: Business Model Generation

Once we had a foothold, my former thesis supervisor and I wrote a book called Business Model Generation, that was inspired by the research I had done for my dissertation, but geared towards a more general audience. We created the kind of book that we would have wanted to buy and read ourselves: one that doesn't just focus on words, but also on form and presentation in order to make the content accessible and aesthetically appealing. That is hard to find in the business book market.

In the writing of Business Model Generation, we tried as much as possible to practice what we preached, and really integrated people who were using the model. We asked them to collaborate with us on the writing of the book, and they paid to do so. In exchange, they were given access to the content first, became part of a community of practitioners, received a copy of the book, and were listed as co-authors. We managed this community on BusinessModelHub.com, a customized Ning.com website, which allows you to build communities.

Charging people to be a part of the project made them feel much more committed. They worked to promote it, and in turn, all of our audiences grew. That barrier to entry reduced the size of the community we could work with, but the end result was of a much higher quality than it would have been otherwise. It has more impact.

Management books have been more or less the same for decades: an article or essay followed by case studies about the topic. Traditionally, these books are long, technical, have too many case studies and not enough directly useable information. I have always disliked this model, and I asked the people in my online community what they liked and disliked about management books. The answer was clear: make them shorter, more visual, and more applicable.

This gave us the opportunity to differentiate ourselves within the business book market, and give our potential readers what they wanted. They responded very positively, and again, our audience grew.

We would never have been able to write this book through a publisher. A four-color design-heavy book would have been too expensive for them to produce and for bookstores (the publishers' main customers) to buy. These are historic, limiting constraints that we were able to get around completely by offering our book directly to the public who wanted it. Later, when the book was a success, we sold the global publishing rights to Wiley. Finally, the book became a top 10 business book in the United States.

Having a book was important to me. Books are still symbolically important. They carry so much more weight than a popular blog or Twitter feed alone. It legitimizes your message and the messages of those you work with, and gives you a strong foundation to work from.

This was particularly true in the case of Business Model Generation; because the book was in and of itself an example of the innovative business models we were talking about. The proof was in the publication and the readership that these new and innovative ideas *work*.

Growing the Business Model Hub

We opened BusinessModelHub.com after publication, and it grew rather chaotically.

Soon we'll be working on applying some structure, but up until now it has been an excellent place to share. Our community members are very engaged, and willing to distribute their knowledge to others in the group. I've found that people are excited to have a place to talk about business models. There was no such dedicated place before, and that fact has increased traffic as well.

There are so many spaces out there on the internet, in almost every industry and sector, which makes the competition for attention a very real issue. Standing out in your field is going to be important. In my case, there were many, many spaces on the internet for talking and sharing about business issues, but none of them were quite the dedicated niche that we wanted to be, which is why we were able to capture the attention of this community.

For me, having an audience has always been about sharing ideas; testing them, getting feedback on them, developing new ones, and to an extent, profit. That's the basis behind the freemium model. Give good content away for free, and generate income with other, related applications.

Currently I'm working on a software company that will be supporting the concepts discussed on the hub and in the book. Some of it will be for free, some of it paid, but all of it will be shaped around the community of business model (innovation) practitioners.

The Audience and the Business Model

The audience is an integral part of our business model, and it will be for yours, too. Is your goal to reach out to them, to acquire them, to sell to them or something else entirely? This question has to be a key part of your business planning from the get-go.

Look at RedHat for example. They've built their entire business model on a community of developers working on Open Source software. They're offering great content for free, providing a place for people to share information and ideas, and have dramatically reduced their fixed development costs.

Sketch out your business model (you can use the canvas on the opposite page, or download a higher resolution version from BusinessModelGeneration.com, and go get my book for help on how to use it!), making a clear point of what your audience will be for, whether its promotion, potential customers, development, support – you name it. Any method of utilizing your audience (while providing value to them!) should be an integral part of your business model.

My own Business Model Hub community of practitioners is very engaged.

I thought that meant that there would be a huge response rate to posts – lots of feedback about ideas, and so forth, but it turned out that only a small percentage of users actually comment on and give feedback about the information I share, but a huge percentage of them absorb the content, and then promote it to other people.

Business Model Canvas

Key Partners	Key Activities	Value Propositions	Customer Relationships	Customer Segments
	Key Resources		Channels	

Cost Structure	Revenue Streams

Until it's happening, you can never be entirely sure of how your audience is going to engage with you. Be prepared to be flexible – meeting your audience's needs is as important as their meeting yours.

I've very recently had my own "Starting from Scratch" experience with a new company that I built with a colleague of mine. It was a consulting firm advising private banks on how to integrate new business models into their operations. Private banking is one of the most conservative fields you can be in, and yet we've got bank managers and other professionals from all over the world participating on our website.

What made this possible was a strong focus on the quality of the design in the website. My other websites have, in the past, looked rather amateurish, despite the fantastic content. With this one we had to back up the fantastic content with amazing design to enhance our credibility, and give our users the confidence in our skills to apply innovative techniques to their industry.

If I could offer you any piece of advice for starting from ground up it would be to make sure that your design, and your presence, is as good as your content.

Dr. Alexander Osterwalder (@business_design) is an entrepreneur, speaker and consultant in the field of innovative business models, and is the author of the global bestseller Business Model Generation.
Start of Audience Building: 2010
Blogs and Websites: AlexanderOsterwalder.com; BusinessModelAlchemist.com; BusinessModelGeneration.com
Publications: Business Model Generation
Our Favorite Blog Post: Reverse Engineering Facebook's Business Model with Ballpark Figures

Brian Clark: Build the Audience, Opportunity Will Come

If you listen, your audience will tell you what to create.

If you want to build an online audience, you've got to teach people something valuable. Or entertain people. Preferably both.

I chose copywriting as the topic I wanted to teach because I was good at it. But more importantly, it's a topic that's central to online marketing that *actually works*.

A good copywriter understands what makes people tick. The principle of writing with the problems and desires of others in mind is the foundation of any successful business.

I came to understand content as a form of marketing by accident. I started out in 1998 by creating and distributing e-zines, which were more or less the blogs of their day. I was delivering good, valuable content to people and at the time, that was newsworthy.

From a marketing standpoint, I had no idea what I was doing. My only goal was to create something valuable and share it with people.

I never really considered what I was doing to be anything *other* than sharing content until I read Seth Godin's "Permission Marketing". Since I didn't really have anything to unlearn when it came to traditional marketing, I was an instant disciple.

Reading the book allowed me to identify what I was doing: content marketing.

Success Comes from Content

From about 2000 to 2005 I ran a very profitable business in the real estate sector, built entirely online and with content as a lead generation strategy. I didn't enjoy running the business, but I loved the marketing and succeeded with a lot of the principles that I write about now on Copyblogger – great headlines, focused landing pages, search engine optimization, and email marketing.

It was time to move on – but to what?

Blogging had caught on by this point, and it was a very logical extension to what I'd been doing – creating and sharing great content. I just didn't want to be in the real estate business anymore.

What I *did* want was to build an audience on my own terms. When you have an audience, you never have to rely on anyone else for your marketing for you, AND people will seek *you* out with amazing opportunities.

There were plenty of blogs out there about blogging, even in 2005, and I didn't want to be just another one of them. I did notice, however, that many of these blogs discussed copywriting issues – titles, structure, calls to action – but they were treating it as if it were something new and unique to blogging.

So I decided to approach blogging and content from the perspective of copywriting. In other words, online content is a form of advertising that attracts people with valuable information, so applying some of the principles of writing for advertising made sense.

It was a broad, wide open niche that I could fill.

I wrote Copywriting 101, which has become a cornerstone 10-part tutorial on Copyblogger. It's several years old now, but it keeps getting more popular all the time. That's because it embodies our philosophy, that certain fundamental principles are going to apply in all online activities, so you'd better get them right.

When you create a piece of content that follows that philosophy, people are going to value it, and share it. That's how marketing within the context of social media works.

Social Media as Word-of-Mouth Content Distribution

For a content marketer, social media is about developing an audience relationship with people who find value in your content, and making it available to them to use and share.

It can be commenting on blogs, voting at a social new site, sharing on Facebook and Twitter, and so on.

Here's the thing: social media doesn't just let you share your content – if used correctly, it can help you figure out *what to create*.

Most of the content that we create on Copyblogger has been inspired by interactions with our readers in the comments that they leave, the questions that they ask, and the emails that they send us.

Social media is this amazing gift to online business people: real-time marketing research. People will come right out and express their problems, desires, and needs without being asked, as long as you take the time to look.

We have people reading Copyblogger who are total novices, and they ask us questions. They're not likely to do business with us anytime soon, but we answer.

Usually, other people are wondering the same things. These are direct clues as to what type of content we should be producing to help people advance. This gives them confidence, and eventually they'll share our content or buy something from us.

Most people's approach to marketing is to start with something they want to sell, and then painfully realizing that people didn't want to buy it.

Social media lets you do a lot of listening before you start talking, and then actually produce something people want and will be willing to buy. I never imagined when I started Copyblogger that I'd be able to turn it into a successful software company, but having the audience allowed me to connect with people who had the skills to create what I, in turn, could sell.

Those relationships are what make all the difference, and you create relationships through engagement.

Why Engagement is NOT Enough

Engagement is a word that I think is very badly overused in the context of online marketing and social media. This is largely due to "gurus" who write books and give speeches about the importance of engagement, but have never sold anything other than books and speeches.

Don't get me wrong. I love blog comments, retweets, Facebook shares and everything else – they're great feedback and let me know what I should be focusing on editorially. And they also spread our content and create exposure for our company.

But engagement can't be the be-all and end-all of any business. The ultimate metric we should be using is *conversion*.

How many of those engaged people are actually buying something from you?

Great content and engagement go hand-in-hand, but we all know someone who has great engagement and no money. There needs to be a tie-in between what you share openly and freely and what you charge money for.

Providing free content is what it takes to reach people, but you can't shy away when it's time to start charging money. It's not true that no one will pay for something if they're used to getting information for free, as long as what you're selling is closely related and of high quality.

You're providing free value by telling a story that leads to a solution that happens to cost money. That's just good business.

Have a Transparent Agenda

You have to plan out what you ultimately want to achieve, and then create a content strategy that gets you there. On Copyblogger, we have an editorial calendar that goes ahead several months, and it culminates in the next product we're launching.

We think about what we need to be doing in the future in terms of giving away great content while also making money by selling great products. And you shouldn't hide this from your audience.

Not every post has an agenda, but every post fits into the overall goal of generating more conversions by creating more value for and trust with the audience.

We give in order to get, and I like to say that I'm empowering my audience enough to do business with us. If I can give someone the skills to create content, then they'll be in a position to use our WordPress designs and software to be even more effective and efficient.

Only a fraction of the people who read Copyblogger actually end up buying something from us, but everyone gets value. In return, there are people who buy, and people who share, and people who do both.

Stop and think for a minute about how amazing that is. Focus on providing value first, and people will spread the word for you, and also become your customers and clients.

We're in a position where we can develop the sophistication of our audience to an extent that they find enough value in our products and services to pay for them. That wouldn't be possible without free content and social media.

Bottom Line: It Works!

We're a multi-million dollar company that's doubling in value every year.

The issue isn't whether or not free content works. It does. The issue is whether you're measuring conversion rather than some nebulous concept of "engagement" via comments, Facebook likes, etc.

Engagement without conversion is useless.

For example, Twitter is a fantastic content distribution platform that serves up fantastic word-of-mouth exposure. At the same time, Twitter is a low-commitment, low trust environment – the opposite of the environment you need to create in order to get people to convert to customer or client.

You need to be grabbing people's attention on social networks and moving them closer to you until they trust you with an email address. Email remains the top online conversion channel, because you've earned their attention.

So you continue to provide valuable free content. Once people give you their trust and receive enough value from you, they'll be ready to say "Okay, I'll do business with you."

You don't have to have a huge audience to be successful at content marketing, and you can start from nothing and build a fantastic business.

If you want to succeed, be the person who builds an audience. Start today.

Brian Clark (@Copyblogger) is the founder of Copyblogger and CEO of Copyblogger Media. He has been a pioneer in content-driven online marketing since 1998, and is one of the world's leading authorities on copywriting.
<u>Start of Audience Building</u>: *2006*
<u>Blogs and Websites</u>: *Copyblogger.com*
<u>Our Favorite Blog Post</u>: *Why People Don't Want the "Real" You*

Danny Brown: Build Your Goals First

Have a laser-focused understanding of who your audience is and what you want from them.

When people think of growing an engaged audience, it's usually in reference to blog readers; or an email list; or visitors to a sales page on your website; or listeners to your podcast; a social network community; or similar.

But what are we really building an audience for?

Is it simply to participate (click through on an offer, or download a product)? Or is it to interact, via comments on a blog, tweets, Google+ conversations and more?

If it's the former, then do you even care about engagement?

After all, no-one says anything on a sales page except the seller, so where would the need for engagement be?

If it's the latter, though, and you're looking to build a truly engaged following, you first need to build your goals for what that engagement will look like, and what the end goal really is.

It Doesn't Need to Be About the Sale

When I first started DannyBrown.me as my main blog, there was no agenda for it to be a lead generation platform. While a lot of business blogs will act as a cover for a sales message (and there's nothing wrong with that), my goal was a bit different.

Instead of having a ton of ads and affiliate links, and subconscious messages to drive traffic to my company website, I simply wanted a place where I could put ideas out, and have others respond to them, no matter whether the response was positive or negative.

There are so many blogs out there that simply state a point of view, and don't encourage further conversation – I found little to get excited about on these blogs.

And I made a decision. While I couldn't guarantee that I'd get a lot of readers, I could guarantee that those who did find me would arrive at a place where their view was just as important as mine, if not even more so.

I'd also keep my viewpoints honest, even if it meant pissing off the leaders in the space that I was blogging about (and it's done this a few times!). Again, this meant that readers would know that they could come to my blog and learn exactly how I feel about something, and they'd have the platform to share their frustrations too, whether they agreed with me or not.

By doing this, I've been incredibly fortunate from the very start to have great conversations in the comments, which have then found their way to social sites (especially my Facebook page, and more recently on Google+).

There may not have been a huge amount of conversation in the beginning, but I stuck to my goal of having an open mic where all opinions are respected equally. I feel that the growth that I've been fortunate to experience has been a direct result of word-of-mouth about opinions being welcome.

Learning As You Go

Of course, like anyone, I've made mistakes along the way, and will probably make more – no one is perfect, after all.

A few of my early posts are the kind I would call "traffic jams" – lots of traffic, but not going anywhere. The list posts; the Top 10 Ways To… posts; the posts about Twitter, or Facebook, or blogging – basically, the posts that were easy to write but had little real substance.

That's not to say that they were written that way deliberately – every post I've written has been with good intent.

But from a satisfaction standpoint , there was little to be had from some of these early publications. I could have easily stayed on that path, and probably had a lot more subscribers than I currently do.

But the likes of Mashable have already got these types of posts covered.

Instead, I wanted somewhere that would be a real source of engagement. So I learned from the easy posts, and made a more conscious effort to write more questioning posts, and try to offer ideas that weren't available elsewhere (at least, not that I could see).

And it worked.

My list of subscribers grew, as did the engagement with my readers. And not just on my own blog – I've been really fortunate to have other bloggers write about something I've written, and then offer a continuation of a comment they may have left, or take the topic into new areas completely.

For someone that thrives on interactivity and engagement, you can't ask for much more than that.

Ch... Ch... Ch... Changes

As I've mentioned, since laser targeting in on the kind of content I wanted to have on my blog – which correlates to the discussions over on my Facebook Page and Google+ – I've never looked back on the level of engagement I'm fortunate to experience.

Comments frequently number over a hundred per post; social shares on Twitter, Facebook, LinkedIn, etc., are also healthy. I couldn't buy this level of respectful debate if I tried.

I'm also honored to have amazing guests writing for me on Mondays. In fact, doubly honored, as I rarely accept requests for guest bloggers; instead, I target those I feel can bring something amazing to me and my readers. Thankfully, everyone has said yes so far – so I guess I'm doubly honored.

I'm a huge believer that the engagement I've encouraged has resulted in the community it's fostered. And that community has been there for me when I needed them.

From defending me against personal attacks on my integrity from a non-profit consultant (which she later apologized for and removed from her blog), to rallying around me when I was seriously ill in 2010, the community around my blog never ceases to amaze me.

That doesn't mean I wouldn't have done anything differently – heck, if we're always satisfied, then we aren't growing! So what changes would I have made?

✓ **I would have posted less frequently.** I started off writing a blog post a day (and sometimes I posted more than once on the same day). Sometimes this made me publish stuff that, in hindsight, could have (should have) been better. In the middle of 2011, I made a conscious decision to post less frequently, and really ask questions of things in the stuff I wrote about. It made me a better blogger, and resulted in the ensuing comments going through the roof.

✓ **I would have been more honest.** Let me rephrase that: I would not have been afraid to speak honestly. There were times early on when I wouldn't have said anything negative about certain people, since I (incorrectly) thought they were right. Turns out we all get blinded by vacuous respect. When I realized this, and began writing openly about bad practices and calling out bullshit, it once again raised the level of engagement through the roof, as others were clearly thinking the same thing. Be honest, and you'll have engagement.

✓ **I wouldn't be so closed off.** One of the things many bloggers complain about is that social sites like Twitter and Facebook have seen comment numbers decrease, as conversations about a post shift there, as opposed to taking part on the blog. Heck, I even wrote a post about Twitter killing blog comments! But that's missing the point – engagement comes in all shapes and sizes, and while your blog may be the most desired place for discussion, true engagement allows the discussion to expand in all directions. If I was to do anything differently, it'd be to get active sooner on Facebook (and now Google+). Because, ironically, I've tended to find that the more willing I am to converse away from my blog, the more likely people are to click through and read more of my stuff. And that's a win-win for everyone.

Never Stop Learning

Will the above work for you as you look to build an engaged community of your own? Maybe, maybe not.

A lot will obviously depend on your blog (or list, or whatever it is you're trying to make more interactive). Going by my analytics, the demographic of my readers is absolutely right for the content I write – so that immediately gives me a boost when it comes to engagement.

I know that when I use the framework of what's worked for me, and the changes I needed to make, with my clients, they enjoy a more engaged audience. So I think the fundamentals might be useful – but don't quote me on that!

One thing that is guaranteed, though, is this: if you want to build engagement, build your learning, and never stop learning.

- ✓ Learn who your audience is.
- ✓ Learn what they want to read.
- ✓ Learn where they prefer to converse.
- ✓ Learn how to be open.
- ✓ Learn that you're never 100% correct.

If you can see where you're going right, and learn to notice where you're going wrong, it'll be easier to take the steps needed to grow your engagement, and keep it growing.

And if you can do that?

Well, you've just laid the first brick in building your engagement model. Now you just need to keep building – but that's the easy part, as long as you know how to be open to growing the right way.

Danny Brown (@DannyBrown) is co-founder and partner of Bonsai International, a prolific blogger on the AdAge Power 150.
Start of Audience Building: 2006
Blogs and Websites: DannyBrown.me, BonsaiInteractive.com, 12for12k.com
Our Favorite Blog Post: How to Kill Your Blog in 10 Easy Steps

Guy Kawasaki: 99 Happy People

Understand and apply the three pillars of enchantment: likeability, trustworthiness, and quality.

I started my career by falling in love with an Apple II.

The fact that I could do word processing was magical at a time when Selectric typewriters with correction tape were the state of the art. Seeing a Macintosh for the first time was a religious experience. Shortly thereafter I became an evangelist for the Macintosh Division, and my task was to convince developers to write software for Apple's new computer.

My success grew with Apple's success; as the saying goes, a rising tide floats all boats. This led to books, speaking engagements, advising, investing, blogging, and finally social media. My first book was *The Macintosh Way*. I wrote it in 1986-1987. The book was rejected by several business book publishers but luckily Scott Foresman, a textbook publisher, believed in me enough to take it to market.

When I began my career, there was no such thing as Facebook or Google+, and Twitter was a noise that birds made. These three platforms have changed marketing forever. Now you can reach billions of people. In the old days of Dale Carnegie, when he wanted to communicate his message, he could reach all of the people in the ballroom. You and I can reach people in every corner of the globe, and we can reach them instantly and inexpensively.

The Three Pillars of Enchantment

The foundation of social media is elements that are timeless – they worked in Dale Carnegie's time, and they still work today. The three elements are likeability, trustworthiness and quality.

Likability. If people don't like you, they're not going to listen to you, let alone purchase your product or service. People prefer to do business with people that they like, so it doesn't take a rocket scientist to see that one of the best ways to develop relationships with your audience is to be likable. You smile when you meet someone in real life, and you can send a friendly greeting when you meet someone online.

Trustworthiness. You must do what you say you're going to do when you say you're going to do it. If you develop a reputation as unreliable, dishonest or questionable, you won't enchant people. You develop trustworthiness by trusting others first, dealing fairly with everyone you meet, and making your conflicts of interest visible to people.

Quality. Arguably the most important of the pillars, everything you produce must be worth reading, buying, or just spending time thinking about. Great products and services are DICEE: deep, intelligent, complete, empowering, and elegant. Think about Apple's products – you want to be the Apple of your market.

Applying the Pillars with Facebook, Twitter, and Google+

Once you have basics down pat, then you can move on to applying social-media tools such as Facebook, Twitter, and Google+. These are fantastic tools that provide a megaphone that you can use to spread your message and develop your business. Unfortunately, "social media experts" cause a lot of confusion and frustration with their Fascist recommendations. It starts with their recommendation that you absolutely must first create a strategy with goals, milestones, and expected results that you can follow, step-by-step, to success.

This is ridiculous.

It's ridiculous because it overlooks the most important part of social media: that they're social, free-flowing, ever changing, and malleable for each person's style. If you were a kid going to a new high school for the first time, would you sit down and plan out a detailed, step-by-step strategy on how to make friends and become popular? Not likely. In fact, it would be pretty scary if you did.

Let me tell you how I use Twitter, Facebook, and Google+. I'm not saying that these are the only ways, or the best ways – only that this how I use them.

Twitter is a link economy. The way to get street cred is to share great content whether it's your own or that of others. I've got hundreds of thousands of followers that are interested in the content I tweet about, because I tweet about things that I find genuinely interesting, and that meet the standards of the three pillars.

Facebook is a picture economy. I use pictures that I post and my readers post to trigger conversations with people, so Facebook is a forum – an engagement and sharing tool where I thread conversations with people. I'm much more proactive in terms of posting content and responding to people on Facebook. It's active for me, whereas Twitter is more reactive.

Google+ is, as of this writing in July 2011, the Wild, Wild West. No one really knows what works on Google+ yet. So far for me, Google+ is Facebook on steroids: post a picture or video and get up to hundreds of comments. Respond to the comments, and you get more comments. I love it.

No Guts, No Glory

Regardless of the platform, set yourself up as a likeable, trustworthy, quality-driven person in your niche. Just dive in by always posting great links, pictures, and video, and then see what happens. As you learn the capabilities and shortcomings of each platform, you'll figure which one serves your needs the best---or maybe they all do in different ways.

Now the question is: Should you follow my advice? You shouldn't believe me any more than you should believe social-media experts. This is what I do – perhaps my practices can help you. Admittedly, I'm an outlier, and I break "established" rules. This may not be something that you can get away with, or maybe, it's what will make you successful. There's only one way to find out.

Guy Kawasaki (@GuyKawasaki) is the author of Enchantment: The Art of Changing Hearts, Minds, and Actions. He is also a public speaker, founder of Alltop.com, and former chief evangelist of Apple.
Start of Audience Building: 1984
Publications: Enchantment; Reality Check; The Art of the Start; Rules for Revolutionaries...
Websites and Blogs: Alltop.com; GuyKawasaki.com
Our Favorite Blog Post: How to Enchant your Customer

Mark W. Schaefer: Community through Tenacity

Building a great community is just the beginning…

By all measures, I have one of the most awesome blog communities on the social web. They tease me, correct me, and even take me to the mat and tangle with me over controversial issues. In other words, we have a lot of fun!

In 2011 I averaged about 60 comments a day and it's not unusual to have 100 or more. And they're not just "Great post Mark!" Many comments are longer, and are more impactful, than the original post!

This is a smart, loyal bunch... one of the most exciting blog communities on the web. How did it happen?

As I reflect on building this community, a few turning points stand out that might help you in your own efforts. At least these are things that have worked for me...

Strike Hard With Originality

When I started my blog, I really had no idea what I was doing. I had a child-like, perhaps even a naive, approach. This was not a mindful act. It started that way because I just jumped in for fun and the sheer joy of experimentation.

So I didn't have a pre-conceived notion of what a blog should be. I did not read a lot of blogs, I wasn't worried about SEO, affiliate links, or being politically correct. I had no expectations about community or page rankings. Like a child, my posts were honest, blind to politics, and playful. It was just a pure expression of what was on my mind. I didn't know it at the time, but this is a rare commodity on the social web. Digging down deep and providing something really different and exciting got the community to notice. Fight "sameness" with your every blogging breath.

Early promotion — I used the old marketing maxim to go where my "customers" are as I began introducing the blog. For example, as I was trying to gain traction, I would use links to blog posts to help answer questions in LinkedIn forums. I was an active participant in other blogs (as I still am) and also made a point to promote the blog every place that I would naturally leave my email address (like a business card, signature line, etc.). I used the blog to be authentically helpful and connect to new people. This advice about building a community is pretty consistent across the social web, and it really is essential!

The first visitors — What a joy and surprise to find people enjoying my blog and even commenting! I made an effort to connect with them by helping to support their blogs – and Twitter efforts, too. Sadly, I have so many regular readers of {grow} that I cannot possibly do this today. The irony of social media is that the result of success is LESS engagement. I really hate that.

Asking for help — It got to a point where I was writing what I thought were really unique posts but they still weren't getting much attention. So I asked for attention. When I wrote something really great, I would send a link to some bloggers I admired and asked them for feedback. This is a euphemism for "a tweet." People are really nice on Twitter and I never had a request turned down. Of course I only asked sparingly and only when I thought I had an extraordinary post. But it helped.

Show gratitude — There is this rumor going around (Gini Dietrich!) that I wrote personal notes thanking people for their help. This is true. That may seem like overkill but I didn't know any better. I was being polite! For example, early in my blogging career Jason Falls wrote a very kind post indicating that I was an up and coming blogger to watch. So I wrote him a thank you note. Why wouldn't I? It's polite but I guess it also helped me stand out.

Taking a human view — Behind every little commenter picture is a story and an awesome person. That fascinates me to no end. I am so hungry to learn more about you! I wish I could know all of you so much better. One of the things that has made a difference is treating people like people, rather than treating them as comments. If I sense that a commenter is struggling or suffering, I invite them to call me. I know that this is seen as "taboo," but the way I see it, we're all in this together, right? Why not help each other when we can? There is no reason we can't be friends.

Being involved — I try to thoughtfully respond to each comment. I think that encourages people to be involved, but it is also a matter of simple courtesy. Every day I am blown away that people spend their precious time commenting on my blog. I think I owe them a response in return – it's the least I can do.

Host a Human Blog

Think about your favorite blog post. I bet it wasn't a list of "Five Biggest Twitter Mistakes". It was probably something that connected to you on an emotional level. Admit you're wrong. Admit that you're tired or confused. Bloggers aren't super heroes. Have the courage to be humble. As writers, and as leaders, there is strength in weakness.

Blog Tenaciously

Readers need both quality AND consistency and that takes a lot of hard work. At the end of the day, insanely great content nurtures a blog community. That's where I started this piece, and it is where I will end it. It seems trite, but it really is true – content is the currency of the social web.

I positively know that people find the blog and stay there due to the content. When I write something great, I am rewarded with comments and tweets. And there are no short cuts – if you want to grow a community, be prepared to put in the hard work to settle for nothing less than consistent, compelling, relevant, and entertaining content.

The Pay-Off

I know I'm supposed to be writing about building a blog community but I would be remiss if I didn't mention the reward of all this hard work...

Sometimes I get weary responding to comments at 2 a.m. I've wondered if I am on the right path. But then I catch a glimpse of an evolution – something exciting happening on {grow}. It is becoming a REAL community. People are connecting and helping each other. They are connecting within my community, and building new value together.

I recently hosted a national social media event called Social Slam that was built almost entirely from my blog community. And let me tell you, when you finally met these folks in real life... and they embrace you like a brother... and they trust you with their life story... and tell you that you have impacted their lives... you begin to realize that even a little blog community can become a movement that is leading to something bigger. I don't know what, but it's going to be bold and amazing.

So building is just the beginning. It can lead to so many business benefits and personal satisfaction. My community has become my customers, my collaborators, my friends. So I'm going to follow my own advice and keep building, because I can't wait to see what happens next!

Mark W. Schaefer (@MarkWSchaefer) is a marketing consultant and college educator and blogger.
Started Audience Building: 2009
Books and Publications: The Tao of Twitter
Blogs and Websites: BusinessesGrow.com/blog
Our Favorite Blog Post: How Social Media Amplifies Competitive Advantage

Mitch Joel: Be Damn Interesting

Your audience does not have to be your client base, but your client base must be a part of your audience.

I started my career in traditional print media, writing about music and entertainment.

Back then, there wasn't really a space where I could express my passion for business and marketing. The advent of blogging and digital communication changed that, and allowed me to create content about the things that I really knew and loved.

Blogging, ultimately, helped me to find and foster an audience.

Most of my writing time goes towards creating content for Six Pixels of Separation. It's where I share what I'm thinking, test new ideas, and engage with other professionals.

The act and the art of writing is how I turn a thought or a theory into something that I can use for our clients at Twist Image. I approach writing as a problem solving and critical thinking exercise more than anything else. For me, learning is a huge part of the writing process, and I find greater clarity and understanding through writing.

90% of my audience consists of people who would never become Twist Image clients, and that's okay.

In fact, it's great, because that 90% is getting something valuable out of my content, and providing something as well: feedback and promotion to the people who might be part of the other 10%, who would actually use my services. When that other 10% see the level of community and interaction I have on the site, it acts as a better validation tool for the quality of my company than anything else could.

The act of creating content, in the form of my blog posts, podcasts and presentations, is a way of exorcising my internal demons and personal challenges –

getting out the thoughts and ideas that would otherwise languish unused in my brain. It's cathartic.

Doing Great Work

When it comes to blogging and audience building, there is one thing that matters more than anything else: *doing great work*.

Everything else follows from that. The process that I described above is how I create great content – you need to figure out your process. Very likely, it will be directly related to *why* you write. If it's sincere, and comes from a place of real passion, the audience will follow.

In the world of blogging, as in the music industry, the cream rises to the top. Once upon a time, bands would play in clubs, hoping that someone important will come in, hear them and sign them to a label. Those days are long gone, thanks to social media. Today artists can make their work widely available, and actually interact with the people they need to in order to gain attention and audience.

The same is true with bloggers. The best of them, creating the best content, will have the most success.

Like every single other blogger on the internet, I am only as good as my audience. My ability to communicate and engage with people is the only thing that limits my message. The more people who think that your work is of real quality, the further your message and ideas will reach. You have to be awesome, or you'll fall flat on your face.

Awesome is...

Unfortunately, "awesome" can't be defined. If someone could pin down - once and for all - the definition of "awesome" they'd be set for life, and the rest of us could stop floundering around trying to figure it out. Everything is subjective. Words, like art or music, will always appeal to some people (hopefully!) and not to others. It's the nature of the business.

Think for a minute about John Lennon's song "Imagine". It's got that irresistible, impossible to pin down quality of "awesomeness" – but why? For the song to be created, Lennon had access to the same seven chords that every other musician access to, and the lyrics are words that all of us use on a daily basis, but it's been a hit from the day that it was released. Something about it connected with people, and made them want to listen to it again, and again, and again. The way the words and melody flowed and were put together created this new form of awesome.

This is the effect that your content needs to have on your audience.

It's Not All About You

There are, of course some standards and rules that can *generally* be applied to the development of an audience, particularly if you're just starting out.

The most important one is that *it's not all about you*. Unless you're in a field so esoteric that no one else is currently blogging about it, there is already an established online community that you're going to be a part of, whether you like it or not. So you may as well get out there and get involved in it!

Comment on the work of other bloggers, and share it with your own audience. Reach out and get to know those bloggers, and they will return the favor. If you add value to their community, they will help you build yours.

Doing this isn't that difficult. Start with two or three blogs and leave comments, offering valuable insights, and people will be curious about you. Use Twitter and Facebook as a means of communicating with your audience; don't fall into the trap of getting people to "like" you and leaving it at that.

Someone "likes" you. So what?

"Liking" is huge right now. Every business wants to get as many "likes" as possible.

But, let's say that someone "likes" you. So what?

Does it mean they're going to seek you out and hire you? Will they go out of their way to share your content? Probably not. For that, you need a real relationship or content so fantastic they can't keep it to themselves. The real usefulness of social media sites comes in when a blogger or business owner can connect directly and have a relationship with their audience.

There are lots of ways to drive traffic and gain readers; paid online advertising, link building, link exchanging and all the different forms of traditional media. But engagement is much more than that.

Look at Dove (and I realize that this example has been beaten to death, but bear with me), for example. They began their advertising traditionally, long before there was any social media to speak of. The touted the qualities of their products – the soap floats, there's not oil, that kind of thing.

When the social media revolution began, they decided to try something different: they started the *Campaign for Real Beauty*, which customers and a whole internet community have taken into their hearts and minds.

That's the relationship you should constantly be trying to develop with your audience. Your audience needs a reason beyond just your product or service to engage with you.

I've been in this business for a long time, the blog has been active for nine years, and during that time I've also been lecturing and creating weekly podcasts. I don't do these things for money, I do them because I love marketing in the digital age.

It's my art, and my blog, podcasts, articles and everything else are my canvas.

 *Mitch Joel (@MitchJoel), called the Rock Star of Digital Marketing, is the creator of the Six Pixels of Separation blog, author of a book by the same name, a prolific writer and speaker, and president of Twist Image, a prominent digital marketing and communications agency.*
Started Audience Building: 2004
Books and Publications: Six Pixels of Separation
Blogs and Websites: TwistImage.com
Our Favorite Blog Post: The Gentle Art of the Retweet

Randy Komisar: An Unlikely Audience

Authenticity is everything.

This might be a different type of essay than many of the others found in this book.

I do no promotion.

I do no blogging, and I am on no social networks.

I don't try to sell my ideas; I put them out there and let people buy them. It's not the best way to do business. If I was business-minded about my ideas – that is to say my writing or speaking engagements – I would take a very different approach.

Until The Monk and the Riddle was published, I had no audience to speak of. I was approached by Harvard Business Press to write the book, and initially, I turned them down. When I finally went back with an idea for a business fable, a business philosophy book, I had no idea it would become so popular. Now that Getting to Plan B is published, my audience has grown even larger, without any real effort on my part. The audience was ready made for me.

Because of this, I had to sit back and really think about what I wanted to do with this audience now that I had it. I realized that I wanted to have a relationship with this audience that went beyond the commercial.

I wanted the ability to share ideas, to stimulate and provoke thinking, to work with others, and to reinvent models – whether they're models of innovation, activity or organization. Because I fell into all of this backwards I've never treated my audience as commercial.

It's important to me that my audience know that I don't take them for granted, that I'm not necessarily selling them anything. The privilege of having an audience is really the privilege of having a wealth of new people to get to know, with whom you can share ideas and work on new ventures.

Creating a Future That You Care About

I've recently written blurbs for three books. These new, young authors approached me and asked for my comments, and because I loved what they were saying and the new ways they were thinking, I reviewed their books. I've been given this opportunity to reinvent myself and accompany them as they move into the future. It's all about creating a future that you care about.

The concept of **a better future** is very important to me. Take investing, for example. You can invest just to make money, but I never do that. When I invest in a business it's because I want to invest my time, my energy, my ideas, and my attention, to help make it something of value. To have positive impact. I need to care very much about who I work with, and who I engage with.

I am humbled, flattered and constantly surprised that I have an audience at all. After I was given the gift of an audience for my first book, I had no reason to believe it would sustain itself, but people have stayed, and more people are coming. I receive more emails and answer more questions about my books now than I did when they were first published. My audience has found an affinity with what I am saying, and we connect based on that affinity.

It's a matter of authenticity. My first book touched so many people because I presented myself to them naked; I had no objectives when I was writing it, commercial or otherwise. I had an opportunity to express myself and my vision, and I expected that I would be able to keep some distance, to maintain some separation. But I could not.

At first my writing partner worked with me on the book more like a shrink than a virtual author. It was difficult, but he pushed me and pushed me until I was ultimately naked. Then I finally felt free to speak honestly and say what I really meant, consequences be damned. To paraphrase Hemingway: "Life is about writing one true sentence." That's what I am trying to do, and an audience is responding to it.

When you try and consciously build an audience, you must ask yourself: to what end? Why do you need an audience?

To what end? Why do you need an audience?

In the age of Twitter, you can create a persona very easily and maintain it for a time – but for what reason? If you lack sincerity, if you can't "get naked" before your audience, eventually they will leave you for someone who will.

When I read new works by many young authors, I have to smile at some of their insights. They seem slightly clichéd to me. But every generation needs to rediscover truths for themselves.

Mine did the same. Those books would not resonate particularly strongly with me if I picked them up off the shelf, but there will be readers who will be exposed to these insights for the first time and experience them as a revelation even if they now seem old hat to me. This is how it should be. As writers and teachers we most often don't invent the truths, we experience them and share them, giving our audience the advantage of "discovering" these insights for themselves. There is some brilliance to regularly reinventing the wheel in order to better understand ourselves – not wheels.

As a writer, I believe that my role is to translate my life experiences into something that other people can relate to. The audience is already out there. They're waiting for you to present them with your insights and the translation of your life experiences so that they might benefit from them. It's up to them to put those insights to work in their own lives.

To use an analogy, in the larger scheme of things, I consider myself more of a character actor than a leading man. If I were a leading man, I'd want the biggest audience possible, but as a supporting player, I have the freedom to be more honest, and to be naked in front of my smaller, more connected and independent group.

There was a time when messages were principally conveyed on soapboxes in town squares. There was a time when it was done by print. There was a time when it was done by radio, then television. Now, it is done by social media. The best part of social media is that it provides free entrance to all – there are no real barriers in the marketplace for ideas. That isn't to say that all users of it are created equal, but everyone does have the same opportunities. There are fewer gatekeepers now than ever before standing in between people and their audience (or potential audience).

So I ask again: why do you want an audience? Is it an ego thing? A vanity play? Is it about numbers or clout? Is it about influence or economics? For me, having an audience is about having an authentic experience and sharing it in an authentic way with people who are tuned in.

That's a word I like: authentic.

I dabbled in the music industry for much of my early career, but in 1970, I could not have told you which artists would have staying power. Looking back, the ones that remain popular and who are still creating music we listen to today are the ones that have lived an authentic experience and shared it with their audience. They live on, and will continue to live on, because their authenticity is something that people can relate to and resonate with personally.

Starting to Build Your Audience from Scratch

You might be reading this because you are just beginning to build your audience – starting to build your audience from scratch. Always, you need to start with content, and then your audience will choose you. If your goal is to create a strong affinity group, something that is bigger than the sum of its parts, your initial challenge lies in getting that content to them. But if you do it right and they welcome you, you can begin the process of creating a better future that you truly care about.

Alternatively, if you take the celebrity route, you could treat your audience as currency, and target them in a commercial way. Some of my businesses do that. They chase an audience and sell advertising or whatnot in order to establish a commercial relationship because it is necessary for them to survive and prosper.

Have you discovered why you want to have an audience yet?

If it's an ego thing, as it is for most people, you'll be counting followers, trying to grow the number as large as possible – it will make you feel important. If gaining more and more followers is your goal then doing so will just continually feed the beast, and soon you'll be increasing your audience only for the sake of seeing it get bigger.

My feeling is that an audience is an affinity group of diverse people with overlapping goals and perspectives. Given that affinity, they have demonstrated what is important to them, and you have an obligation to meet their standards. They aren't "followers", they are participants. And if they are truly engaged they will feel as free to disagree as agree.

In this day in age you can test the waters of your audience immediately as you create things. They will let you know what works and what doesn't. If you're true to your beliefs and value systems and respect your audience as the privilege they are, the feedback you will regularly receive, good or bad, is a precious gift.

I've been carried forward in my career by likeminded writers, teachers and speakers. My audience has become theirs, and theirs has become mine. This is the opportunity that having an engaged audience affords you. To share ideas, experiences and insights. Do not waste it.

Always remember that you have a choice to make about your audience. You can seek to develop affinity, to think and work and share together, or you can use your audience as an economic system. It is very hard to do both.

Randy Komisar is a partner at Kleiner Perkins Caufield & Byers, a popular speaker and business mentor, and the author of the bestselling books The Monk and the Riddle and Getting to Plan B.
Start of Audience Building: 2000
Books and Publications: The Monk and the Riddle, Getting to Plan B
Websites and Blogs: KPCB.com

Stuart Mills: There Is No Set Path

There is no "one-size-fits-all" way to build an audience.

Every blogger in the world today, irrespective of nationality, gender, culture, or age, seeks just one thing.

They want someone to listen.

No matter what the size of their blog – whether they have 10 subscribers or 100,000 – a blogger will seek an audience that is willing to listen, and is engaged with what the blogger is writing, or saying. Without that audience, there is no reason to blog – the blogger may just as well write their "8 Ways To Get More Comments" in his or her diary and file it away.

The audience is the heartbeat, the very essence of blogging.

If there's no audience, there is effectively no blog. Why blog if no one is listening?

With that in mind, it makes sense that finding someone who willingly listens is the key goal for bloggers. That one listener can then become five, and then ten, then a hundred, and so on, but the first priority for the new blogger is to find that first listener.

The Illusion of the Set Path

So, how do you find that willing listener?

That engaged audience who will happily come back to you even after you've sent them elsewhere with a "10 Bloggers You Should Follow" post? Well, I'll share a secret with you. *The* secret. The *secret of blogging*. Are you ready to hear it? Are you sure? Okay, here it is:

There is no set path.

I'm sorry if that comes as an anti-climax, but it *is* the truth, and it *is* a secret.

It's a secret because no-one wants to talk about it, and it's the truth because, well, it's true. There is no set path to achieve that engaged audience that every blogger dreams of. There is no set of rules, or magic code, or 5-step process. What works for one blogger may not work for another blogger, and it may work for a third blogger, yet not work for a fourth blogger.

Leo Babauta of Zen Habits has one of the most popular blogs in the world, with over 200,000 subscribers. He has a large, engaged audience, and so, everyone wants to know how he got it, and what they should do to get that size of audience for themselves. To Leo's credit, he doesn't advise a set path, and says that certain things will only work for certain people. But he has still, possibly due to popular demand, given out advice on growing an audience.

Now, some of this advice has worked for me, and some of it hasn't. I won't say what, but rest assured that the same will very likely be true for you. For example, one of Leo's suggestions is guest posting. It's worked wonders for some bloggers, like Onibalusi of YoungPrePro, but it hasn't worked so well for other bloggers. And others dislike the whole idea of guest posting. Another of Leo's suggestions is to write catchy headlines. Again, this works wonders for some bloggers, while other bloggers stick to the standard "8 Ways To…", "10 Steps To…", and still get plenty of traffic and attention.

So, if one of the largest blogs in the world isn't able to *guarantee* you a set path to reaching an engaged audience, what's the use of asking any other blogger out there? Sure, you could continue your quest by visiting blogs like Problogger and Copyblogger, who each have over 100,000 subscribers and offer plenty of tips and advice, but even they can't offer you a set path. No one can. If you're looking for someone else to show you the path, then I'm afraid you will be disappointed.

To get an engaged audience, you have to figure it out for yourself.

Cross-Referencing

Having said all this, I don't want you to feel disheartened.

No, there isn't a set path, but that doesn't mean you're on your own. Others have walked the kind of path that you wish to walk, and have engaged audiences numbering in the thousands. They've learned a lot about gaining and maintaining engaged audiences, and you can learn valuable lessons from them as you set out to do the same.

It's useful to think of this as cross-referencing.

In any field, when we look at someone who has achieved success that we want for ourselves, we look at what they did and how they did it. Now, by copying what they did to the letter, it's likely you won't experience the same level of success that they did. You may experience less. But if you take what you can in terms of simple 'tips and advice' – if you cross-reference your own journey against theirs and see if there's anything you can learn – you're more likely to succeed.

Why? Because you're not taking everything they did for granted. You're learning your own techniques, your own methods, and if someone else did something that you agree with, feel free to do it yourself. If you disagree with it, discard it.

This is the art of cross-referencing in action – seeing what you can gain from someone else's experience, using what is useful, and discarding what isn't. This way, you get the best of the best, and can develop a path forged by your own experiences and tempered with the advice of others.

What I Can Do

I'm aware that, so far, I haven't given you any advice as to how you might build an engaged audience. This is deliberate, as I wanted to explain to you the simple fact that there is no easy way.

But having said all this, and in the hopes that you've taken the message to heart, I can now dispense *a little* advice to help you build your empire.

Before I begin, I want you to be aware that some of this advice *hasn't* worked for me. The majority of it has, but I've tried some of the advice which I'm about to mention, and I didn't experience any success. I include this advice because I'm confident that even though it didn't work for me, *there's still a chance it will work for you*.

As I said earlier, everyone is different, and what works for one may not work for someone else. So some of the advice that I list that worked for me, may not work for you, and some of the advice that I list that didn't work for me, may work for you. I really don't know. All I can say is to keep an open mind, and try it if it seems like it will work.

Get Out There

A key regret that I have from my early days of blogging is that I didn't venture over to other blogs often enough. I stopped 'at home' and expected people to find me. Instead of getting myself out there, I blindly relied on Google and other search engines to bring up my website in the first few pages when you search for 'personal development blogs'.

Needless to say, this didn't work.

When you're starting out, and you want people to come to you, one of the best things that you can do is go to them. Head out and meet new bloggers, read their posts, and leave a comment if you feel ready to. When you enter the field, you're striding into the busy blogging space, attempting to connect with other bloggers. If you 'stay at home', and prefer to keep producing posts without letting anyone know about them, then no one will know you're even producing those posts. And that means no one will get to read them.

So get out there more, learn to say "hi" to new faces, and start getting into relationships. One such way of introducing yourself, which I wish I knew when I was first starting out, is to leave an 'introductory comment'. For example:

"I just wanted to say that I think you're doing a great job with your blog. I'm new to blogging, and I'm still figuring things out. If you have any tips or advice, I'd really appreciate it. Thanks."

Combine this with a little bit about the content of the post, and you have an introductory comment. This kind of comment shows that you have been paying attention to the blogger (meaning you're an engaged listener!), and that you value their opinion. The results are usually favorable; bloggers love helping others, and will often help a fellow blogger out, especially if they're new.

Use Social Media

Social media seems to be all the rage these days, and with good reason. The likes of Twitter, Facebook, and Google+ can lead you to hundreds and thousands of interested readers, and can help spread work to the furthest corners of the globe. This is very powerful indeed, so it makes sense to use it as much as possible, right?

Yes and no.

I say "yes", because the potential to attract an engaged audience with social media is very large. But I say "no", because it can be very easy to get bogged down by the mass of social media. Social media is a tool, and it's important not to let that tool take over the running of your life.

The social media platforms I use are Facebook, Twitter, Digg, StumbleUpon, and LinkedIn. I have experimented with others in the past, like Reddit and Delicious, but have since ditched them because they were just too much. I became overwhelmed by the scope and size of social media, so I chose to trim it down. I choose to limit myself to a maximum of five platforms – if I encounter a new social media platform that's just too good to miss, I'll ditch one I'm currently using to make way. Otherwise, I'll stick with what I've got.

Social media is there to help you, not hinder you. If you can get good results from social media, then use it for as much and as long as you can. But if you find yourself losing control of the whole situation, and if you're spending more time on social media than your blog itself, take steps to minimize. Your own work must always come first.

Write 'Wantable' Content

Bloggers love the freedom to write whatever they want. This isn't bad, but when you're trying to attract an audience to your blog, it might make sense to create content that is likely to attract an audience. It might make sense to write 'wantable' content to satisfy your readers.

I have struggled to decide whether this works for me. I have written posts that my audience has asked for, and they have been successful. Not always, but often. And yet, I have written posts that have been about what I want to write, and they still attracted an engaged audience, that praised me for being 'original'.

With this advice, there are no set rules. The main thing to ensure is that your content remains interesting and engaging. *An engaged audience needs engaging content*. But what content will that be? It's up to you. Your guess is as good as mine.

Expand Your Reach

It makes sense to focus on your own niche when it comes to networking, so that you can develop like-minded relationships, right? Not necessarily. It may benefit you to reach out into new niches.

Not too long ago, I completed a series titled "Value 101", where I asked 67 bloggers one question: "How do you provide value?" Although my blog is in the personal development niche, I asked bloggers from a wide range of niches, including virtual business lifestyles, content marketing, entrepreneurship, social media, marketing, SEO developments, and blogging tips. I deliberately mixed it up so that I could gain a wide variety of answers, but there's also an added benefit to this approach – you get to meet new people who you wouldn't have met before.

If I hadn't have expanded my reach, and if I had stayed within the personal development field, I wouldn't know 60-65% of the bloggers that I do today. I have intentionally visited blogs on entrepreneurship, marketing and outsourcing in order to meet people who are involved in a different niche than I am, but with whom I could still develop a relationship. And it's been of great benefit, as I've learned things about blogging that I wouldn't have otherwise learned. Sometimes, all you need to find the right answer is a different perspective.

I believe this is a good reason to broaden your horizons, as you never know who else is out there, just waiting to meet someone like you.

To Conclude

I said it at the start, and I'll say it again – there is no set path.

I could give you much more advice than I have done here, but it ultimately wouldn't matter. All that does matter is that you make your own path and discover for yourself what works and what doesn't.

Your blog and your audience are your own, and no one can tell you how to grow them. Now get out there and find that audience!

Stuart Mills (@StuartMillsUTD) is a personal development blogger who wants to help you improve at life. He thinks you're awesome. You can often find him at Unlock The Door, where he writes constantly to make it a better day for everyone.

Start of Audience Building: 2008

Blogs and Websites: UnlockTheDoor.net

Our Favorite Blog Post: Redundancy and the Things it Brings

Section 2: Know and Love Your Audience

Now that we know what we're doing and why we're doing it, it's time to forget about it, and focus on the audience that you're looking to build: knowing them, and loving them – because if you don't, nothing else will work.

Anita Campbell's contribution, "Engaged Community, from Scratch", explains that online communities revolve around shared interest, and you need to know who your audience is, and what they want.

Marlee Ward's essay, "How to Suck at Building an Engaged Audience", teaches that you have to nurture your audience for it to grow.

Tristan Higbee's article, "All You Need Is Love", shares his view that all you need is love… love is all you need. ;)

Without further ado, let's get to it… why growing an engaged audience, from scratch, is all about knowing, and loving, your audience.

Anita Campbell: Engaged Community, from Scratch

Online communities revolve around shared interest; know who your audience is, and what they want.

How do you build an engaged audience?

On one level, the answer is incredibly simple: engage them. But as with anything in business, the devil is in the details.

It's easy to bandy about concepts like engagement and community. What's hard is identifying and executing the many components and steps needed to take an idea inside your head and turn it into something real outside your head.

In other words, if you want to build a community, it takes a long list of strategies and tactics to make it happen.

For clarity of terminology, I am going to refer more frequently to "community" than "audience". Community implies active participation and multi-way communication, whereas audience suggests much more of a one-way communication. People feel less engaged if everything goes in just one direction.

Community can live offline and online. Most of my experience is in creating online communities. So today I plan to explore with you how to create a thriving online community. I will assume that you have already considered the reasons behind your decision to develop an online community. You have a clear objective in mind for how that community will benefit your business. Having decided that, then the question becomes "how do you get started?"

Here are 5 lessons that I've learned for how to engage your audience and build an online community, starting from scratch:

1. Start with a Clear Definition of Your Ideal Target Audience

It's a simple step, but one that often gets overlooked. Who is your target audience, really?

Take the time to figure this out, and have a clear picture in your mind – and the rest of the community-building steps will fall into place. Start with a vague or poorly-defined target audience, and the results won't be nearly as good. After all, how can you know if you're serving your target audience if you didn't know what they were to begin with?

A simple way to define your target audience is to sit back and think of your ideal community member – i.e., the person you want to join your community. Take out a piece of paper or open a Word document on your screen, and list as many details as possible about your ideal reader or participant.

If your ideal target audience is a consumer, list things such as:

- ✓ Age
- ✓ Gender
- ✓ Location
- ✓ Education level
- ✓ Occupation
- ✓ Title
- ✓ Annual income
- ✓ Interests
- ✓ Hobbies
- ✓ Needs as they relate to whatever you provide (e.g., needs inexpensive clothing designed specifically for a unique hobby)
- ✓ Wants (e.g., wants someone to discuss hobby-specific questions with in the evenings)
- ✓ Relationship with you and your business: member of the public; past customer; prospective customer; member of an association; alumni.

If your ideal target is another business, list things like:

- ✓ Industry
- ✓ Type of business
- ✓ Location
- ✓ Size of business in annual revenues
- ✓ Number of employees, if any
- ✓ Title of the community member

✓ Demographics of the community member (age, gender, etc.)

✓ Needs

✓ Wants

✓ Relationship with you and your business: customer; prospective customer; business partners; member of the public; peers; competitors (or not)

After going through this exercise, you should end up with something like this:

"My ideal community member is a man aged 24-44, located in the United States, with at least some college and an income over $75,000, who works as an advanced professional such as a CPA or lawyer, or who works in an executive level position, who can't wait to get out from behind a desk on weekends and go sail surfing, and has enough disposable income to spend at least $5,000 annually on his hobby, who looks for high-quality yet reasonably-priced gear, and during the week goes online to seek information about sail surfing and to connect with other sail surfers and share experiences."

Or for a business-to-business customer, you might end up with something like this:

"My ideal discussion board member represents a small business with 1 to 10 employees, with at least $1 Million in annual revenues, located in any English-speaking country, in a consulting or knowledge (e.g., software, design, or media) industry. The actual forum participant will be a mid-level manager or mid-level professional, male or female, relatively young (under 35) still climbing their career ladder, seeking information to help him or her become a thought leader, and seeking networking connections with others in the field. This is a customer and partner community, and caters to those companies who already have a customer relationship or a partner relationship with my business."

What you're doing is painting a picture of your ideal community member – the more detailed and specific, the better. This doesn't mean that every community member has to fall within your definition of the ideal, or else you're going to boot them out. It just means that this is the ideal community member you have in your mind's eye (and in your launch plan) as you begin. You're going to want to make your community attractive to and appeal specifically to this ideal target.

If others who fall outside of your ideal target join, that's fine. You may even adjust your definition of who is "ideal" as you go along. That is part of the learning process of understanding who your target community really is.

If this exercise sounds similar to defining your target market and customer, that's because in many ways it is. You're defining who it is you intend to serve with your online community.

More importantly, if you've done a proper job, you have defined what motivates people to join and participate in a community. We'll come back to this uber-important point in a few minutes, in point 3 below.

2. Decide Where Your Community Will Reside Online

"Community" can be a broad concept. But I think you will bring greater focus to your efforts if you instead think in concrete terms of a place or places online where your community resides. We're fortunate today that we have so many choices for where to host and build a community.

Social media platforms like Facebook, Twitter, YouTube and Google Plus offer the advantages of a ready-made audience. People are already participating on such platforms. So you may find it easier to attract community members there, than to a site of your own. You're meeting them where they want to congregate.

Consider the downsides, however. If the social platform changes its rules or falls out of vogue, then you could find yourself out of luck. Your community might have been quick to assemble, but it can be just as quick to desert if the social platform is no longer the "in" place. And you may not be able to export contact data to connect with them elsewhere.

Software on your own domain also is an option. This could include solutions like Ning, BuddyPress (combined with a WordPress blog) or a popular forum software such as VBulletin. You will have the most control of your destiny on a site you own. You can monetize your community better on your own site, through sales, than you can on social media. However, you may need to work harder to make others aware of your community.

One common strategy is to combine both approaches. Develop a series of community outposts on various social media platforms. This is how you can draw people, by reaching out to them on the social platforms they already participate in. Then find ways to draw those community participants back to your home base community that you have more control over, on your own domain.

3. Remember: It's Not About YOU!

The most common mistake I see with attempts to develop online community is in thinking everything revolves about *you*. Nothing could be more wrong.

Don't mistake me. Your community may love to hear what you're thinking, what's happening in your life, new initiatives your business is working on, how that product launch went, that new book you just wrote, or other details – but only in moderation.

Moderation is the operative word. Some personal details and inside-the-business information make things interesting. But your audience doesn't want to be on the receiving end of endless updates about you or your business. That's a news feed, not a community.

Communities are about people. People like to:

✓ Talk, not be talked at
✓ Talk about themselves
✓ Talk about what interests *them*

If you can't see a way to shape a community around something beyond you, then prepare yourself for limited or no success. Unless you're a true celebrity, there probably isn't enough interesting information about your life or your business to hold people's interests on a steady diet of nothing but *you, you, you*. Sure, we're fascinated with even the tiniest details about movie stars and TV personalities. But most of us aren't famous celebrities. (And no, your 50,000 Twitter followers don't qualify you as a celebrity.)

You may create a highly successful online discussion board centered 100% around your products. Just don't kid yourself. It may be successful as a technical support forum – but it won't be a community.

So if a community isn't 100% about you or your business, what is it about?

A community has to revolve around a shared interest or a shared motivation. It has to meet some want or need (or both) that the community members have. It can be a hobby. In a business context, it can be information that professionals need to improve business results. It can be about the opportunity to meet and network with like-minded entrepreneurs. It can be about raising a family. It can be about sports. It can be about a certain lifestyle, such as sustainable living or world travel. It can be about health matters, such as a rare disease or chronic condition. The sky's the limit – but it needs to be about something that motivates your ideal community member to share and discuss.

Let's take the example of Facebook. Does this mean you can't build a community around the Fan page for your business? Of course not.

But it means that what you place on that Facebook Fan page, and how you interact with your Fans, had better be about more than you pushing *you* all day, everyday. For example, you'll want to:

✓ Engage people to participate on your Fan page by running polls or asking open-ended questions on subjects they may be interested in, that get them talking.

✓ Share information and insights from sources other than your own blog or website – be a source of information that isn't always about you or coming from you.

✓ Avoid constant sales pitches for your products (selling is not the same as building a community).

✓ Highlight and talk about them – the Fans – when possible, such as by recognizing certain Fans.

✓ Offer special content they can't get anywhere else, that satisfies their interests and motivations.

Keep the focus on community members – and not on you. When you focus on the community members, it becomes much easier to think of the right tactics to build and sustain a community on Facebook. Or anywhere else.

4. Don't Fight Newton's Law of Inertia – Harness It!

What does a 17th century physicist have to do with growing a community? A lot!

Sir Isaac Newton was the first to identify the law of inertia.

The law of inertia roughly states that an object in motion tends to stay in motion, and an object at rest will remain at rest – unless there's intervention of some other force. It means that the natural tendency of something is keep on doing whatever it's doing. If it's not moving, it takes extra effort to get it moving. If it's already moving, the momentum tends to continue unless something else interrupts it.

So let's translate that into the world of online communities.

First 6 months: At first you'll have to exert extra effort to get your fledgling community off the ground.

How many forums or Ning sites have you seen where there are 4 members, and one discussion thread months old – and the community organizer nowhere to be found? When you see a community that is dead on arrival, it's a symptom of a missing-in-action community organizer. It's up to the organizer of a community to shake up the inertia to get that community off the ground. It won't happen on its own.

Don't underestimate the time and effort it will take to launch your community. The first 6 months usually require intensive and extra effort. Depending on the nature of your community and your rate of progress, it could take longer than 6 months.

At a minimum you'll need:

✓ **A marketing plan for how to make your target audience aware of the community.** Ditch the "build it and they will come" mentality. Most of the time that only works in the movies. Make sure you have a plan for how to make your target audience aware of your community. Whether it's blog posts, tweets, press releases, personal invitations to join, participating on others' Facebook pages, email broadcasts, cross-promotions with related communities, or other methods – make sure you plan out and execute your marketing.

✓ **A community leader.** The community leader or manager may be an employee in your organization. Or it may be you. Or it may be a part-time contractor you hire for a few hundred dollars a month. But someone needs to be responsible for getting the community off the ground. If everyone has responsibility, it means no one is really responsible.

✓ **Extra engagement effort.** You'll have few members at first to sustain the conversation, so the community manager or leader needs to fill the void. You may even need to prime the pump frequently, by starting discussion threads and commenting more frequently than normal.

✓ **A team of moderators or other key members you can count on to participate daily or several times a week.** Moderators not only keep an eye out to make sure any community rules are met, but they serve to get the discussion going and keep it going. If the moderators happen also to be well-known in the niche you serve, their reputations can help attract new members. You may need to pay moderators or offer them special perks (such as higher visibility in the community by way of free ads or enhanced profiles) to entice them to participate.

Ongoing: Once the community is off the ground and develops its own momentum, then it's a question of not allowing anything to interrupt its growth momentum.

This may sound like you can be hands off, but that's not so. An engaged audience and community requires active shepherding. Communities, like rental properties, do not thrive under neglectful leaders.

You still must be actively involved in the community you create. The nature of the challenge changes a bit, though, as a community gains its own momentum. You won't need to put such intensive effort into getting people to participate and keeping things going. Instead your focus can shift to deepening the quality of the engagement and the value participants' experience.

Give It Time

Building an engaged community doesn't happen overnight. Think of it as a startup. One of the biggest myths in startup businesses is the overnight success. But overnight successes are incredibly rare. And even most of those we think of as overnight successes or fast risers, took longer to gain a mass audience than we realize.

Many people are surprised to learn that Starbucks, today a household name, has actually been around 40 years, since 1971. How many of us were even aware of Starbucks back in 1982, when it was already 11 years old? Not many. It had just 5 stores that year. The company was in business 21 years before it went public, and 25 years before it expanded outside of North America.

And that's the point. Many of the brands that we think of as overnight successes or fast growth businesses operated in relative obscurity for years before they become widely known. Widespread success didn't happen overnight. It only seems that way, because that's when they first hit our radar screens.

If you constantly compare your startup community against all those mythical overnight successes, it's bound to not measure up! Just say no to the lure of overnight success comparisons.

My advice is: "Dream big dreams – set small goals."

Dream big as a community founder – dream how large and active you want your community to be in 3 or 5 years. Dreams are powerful.

But set monthly goals and focus on meeting those smaller goals. Instead of focusing on growing to 10,000 Fans in one fell swoop, set a more modest monthly growth goal, say, adding 120 rabidly-satisfied Fans each month, and retaining 98% of existing Fans. And focus on more than just community size – it's not just about how big the community is, but how active. For instance, set engagement goals, for how much and what type of activity your Fans participate in monthly.

Achievable goals will keep you moving in the right direction. You won't get discouraged if you don't achieve your Big Dream overnight. By meeting and better yet, exceeding, smaller monthly goals, you'll get a sense of accomplishment and develop confidence. Each month you will get positive reinforcement. This keeps you from succumbing to the discouragement of "overnight success syndrome."

Building an engaged audience, or community as I prefer to call it, is not a small undertaking. I won't kid you. It takes dedication and resources – time certainly and to some degree money.

But it's achievable for businesses of all sizes – from the solo entrepreneur on a bootstrapped budget all the way up to Fortune 100 companies. New communities are being started every day. Don't wait to start yours.

Anita Campbell (@SmallBizTrends) is the CEO of Small Business Trends and BizSugar.com.
Start of Audience Building: 2005
Blogs and Websites: SmallBizTrends.com; BizSugar.com
Our Favorite Blog Post: Entrepreneurial Quotes to Inspire and Inform You

Marlee Ward: How to Suck at Building an Engaged Audience

You have to nurture your audience for it to grow.

Yes, you read that correctly. This article is about how to suck at building an engaged audience online.

Why?

Because sometimes it's easier to see what you should do in business and life by looking at the things you *shouldn't*. If you turned the page expecting to find a neat and tidy recipe for getting people to love you and send you money (and possibly their panties) – this isn't it.

Instead, what follows is a clear-cut guide on how to royally screw up any potential you might have at building a loyal following as an entrepreneur or blogger.

Implement these tips at your own risk! ;)

1. Establish a Blog without Any Specific Purpose

When I first started blogging at MarleeWard.com, I was experimenting. It was a place for me to share my thoughts on life and business. I didn't write with an audience in mind, and I hadn't decided on a specific purpose for my content. I was just "putting it out there." As a result, I had very little success in engaging visitors on my site.

It wasn't until I had absolute clarity about *why* I was publishing content on MarleeWard.com that I started connecting with my audience in a meaningful way. Once I knew exactly *who* I was serving, and *how* I could serve them, my audience truly started engaging with me. Understanding why I wanted to share my message, and who I wanted to share it with, was the catalyst for authentic engagement.

Simply put, you cannot build an engaged audience without first identifying your purpose for doing so.

2. Try to Appeal to as Many People as Possible

According to the International Ice Cream Association (yes, it is a real organization), the most popular (and my personal favorite) flavor of ice cream is good old vanilla. Apparently, vanilla ice cream has been the most popular of all ice cream flavors throughout history. But let me ask you, how often do you hear people raving about an incredible cup of plain vanilla ice cream? I'm guessing it's not that often.

In just the same way that vanilla ice cream appeals to the masses, but gets very little attention, your content will also go unnoticed unless it speaks to one specific person. And I mean just *one* person. So sticking with our ice cream analogy, this means you need to speak directly to the person who loves "goat cheese with cognac fig" flavored ice cream. And yes, that is a real flavor made by Jeni's Splendid Ice Creams.

When you learn to speak your audience's language, they can't help but talk back. Make it your mission to communicate the shared vision, message, or passion you have with your audience. When you share a purpose or a passion with your audience, engagement follows *naturally*.

3. See What You Can Get Your Audience to Do for You Right Away

There is this tiny little law in psychology that carries massive implications. It's called the "Law of Reciprocity." Popularized by psychologist Robert Cialdini, the law of reciprocity basically states that people will be eager to help you when you have helped them first.

So you want your audience to support you, support them FIRST!

By making the people you serve the primary focus of your work, you'll get double in return. If you are going to give, give sincerely. The law of reciprocity will take care of the rest.

4. Don't Take an Interest in Your Readers as Individuals

Replying to reader's comments, and making connections on social networks, has become the norm for beginning bloggers and entrepreneurs who hope to build an engaged audience. But if you really want to kick your level of engagement and influence up a notch, focus on building *real* relationships with your first 15 connections.

Take the time to learn who they are, what they do, and why they like your work. Email them personally, and engage with them privately. Sincerely "give a crap" about them as individuals. If you do this, you'll establish a bond with your audience that is not easily broken.

5. Refrain from Showing Too Much of Who You "Really" Are

This is the part of engaging your audience that is actually a lot like dating. You know the story: you start dating someone, and she's on her best behavior; so you end up head over heels and things go perfectly… for about a month. Then your potential match made in heaven reveals a side of herself you'd wished you hadn't seen and – within two weeks – you guys are Splitsville.

Why? Because Ms. Hot n' Perfect wasn't who she appeared to be! And now you feel like you don't know her, trust her, or even like her. If you don't want your audience to flee the moment you get "real", you need be thoughtfully transparent from the get-go.

Generally speaking, you will attract people who share or relate to your perspective, philosophies, interests, and experiences in some way. If you hold back from giving your audience something that they can connect to – they won't.

6. Make Sure Everything on Your Blog is About You and Your Business

Have you ever been to a networking event where you spot a guy hopping from person to person, speaking loudly about himself and his business, slapping business cards in the slightly closed hands of the people enduring his pitch? Yes, you probably have. And what did you do? Vanish from his line of sight, right?

Nobody *wants* to engage with that guy. In fact, nobody *cares* about that guy. And if you want your audience to engage with you on your website, you can't be *that* guy.

Yes, it is your business and your blog. And you should promote your products and services appropriately. But the real reason people will come to your business or your blog is because of what you can offer, which means your content needs to be about *them*. It needs to help them, teach them, inspire them, and empower them. When you equip your audience with whatever they need to be empowered, you lift them up… and in the process establish an even stronger connection to them.

Sarcasm Aside…

Articulating these insights has been very easy for me in hindsight. But for the most part, I've gathered this understanding, and developed an engaged audience, organically – simply because I engage with visitors to my site just as I engage with visitors to my home or office (which are one and the same, in case you were wondering).

Developing an engaged audience is not a one trick pony. Just as you must tend to a garden for it to grow, you must tend to your audience the same way. You need to know what they want, and how they want it. Then, you must give it to them. If you fail to do that, you leave your audience high and dry, and eventually they will leave you for someone who "gets" them. Get it?

The bottom line is that building an engaged audience rests upon being able to connect people to you, to your message, and to one another. Focus on doing that, and the rest will fall into place.

Marlee Ward (@marldble) is a business and marketing coach who helps solopreneurs build thriving businesses that bring them personal fulfillment. An attorney turned entrepreneur, her mission is to help others do work they are meant to do – just as she has.
Started Audience Building: 2009
Blogs and Websites: MarleeWard.com
Favorite Blog Post: 51 Online Business Ideas for Female Entrepreneurs

Tristan Higbee: All You Need Is Love

All you need is love... love is all you need.

You know, The Beatles were really on to something.

Sure, they churned out tons of awesome songs, changed rock and roll, and made a bazillion dollars, but those catchy tunes also offer sage words of wisdom for Internet marketers.

After blogging for more than 8 years now, I've realized that building a loyal and engaged audience really boils down to two things: loving your people, and making people love you.

It's just like The Beatles said... *Love is all you need.*

Love Your People

Think of your website as a store that's just opened.

You, the store owner, should be in front of the store shaking hands, striking up conversations with passers-by, and inviting people in to see what you've got to offer. Once they come into the store, make sure they find everything they need, and offer them assistance and suggestions as necessary. Help them find just what they're looking for. When they leave, thank them and invite them back.

It's this kind of interaction that brings you new customers, and earns you loyal repeat customers. This is also the kind of thing that gets you a captive audience.

In the early days of your online presence, of course you won't have much of an audience to love. That's OK. You need to make sure that the experience of those who do stop by is a positive one. Regardless of audience size, you've got to show them you care.

Though you can't shake the hands of the people that stop by your site, you can (and should) reply to every comment that people leave. If it's someone's first time on your blog, say hi to them and welcome them. Be prompt in replying to emails, and answer them all.

If someone leaves a particularly awesome comment, shoot them an email and say thanks. Email your top commenters, or those people that have shared your stuff the most at the end of every month, and thank them. See if there's anything you can do for them.

Interact with your readers, even when they're not on your blog, or Facebook page, or whatever. Go comment on their blogs. Chat with them on Twitter or Google+. Like and comment on their YouTube videos.

Do favors for people. Be generous with your social media sharing. If someone emails you and asks you to retweet a post, do it. Link to other people's blogs and blog posts in your content. The amount of goodwill this creates will amaze you.

The more you do all this for others, the more they'll do it for you. Not only will this help build a devoted audience, it will also increase your traffic and strengthen the relationships between you and other bloggers. Your community will be stronger as a result.

Make People Love You

There was a girl named Emily in my 6th grade social studies class. We usually sat a couple chairs away from each other. For some reason, Emily had a crush on me. I don't think I ever talked to her, probably because I was still mildly terrified of girls at the time. Toward the end of the year, she slipped me a note. It said, "I think I love you. Do you love me? Yes or No." And then I was supposed to put a checkmark next to either the yes or the no. The answer was no, but I was so shocked and mortified that I never returned her note and just avoided her part of the classroom for the rest of the semester.

Loving someone is only half the battle; that's the easy part. The trick is getting someone to love you back.

Making people love you is the holy grail of everything.

When people love you, they will respect what you have to say. They will trust you. They will engage with you. They will want your help and seek your opinion. They will share your content. They will buy from you.

So how do you make people love you?

There are a few different ways. In my opinion, the first, best, and most important way is to create unique content. Unique content adds bulky muscle onto the wire frame that is your blog and your Internet presence. And in the battle with other bloggers and content creators in your niche for more readers, the more muscle, the better.

The thing is, most blogs suck.

They're boring. They're all providing the exact same content, and it's usually not even said in a different way. In order to stand out in the crowded blogosphere, you need to provide unique content that people haven't already seen a bazillion times before.

You can create unique content by:

- ✓ Conducting case studies
- ✓ Interviewing people
- ✓ Covering a topic from a new angle (Note: This one is often abused. For example, I don't know how many "How blogging is like X" posts I've seen. But the thing is, no one cares if you can create a shallow analogy relating one thing to something else. Sure, maybe no one has a written about how blogging is like Indian food, but you're still not really covering new territory. You're just doing what everyone else is doing, and doing it just as uninterestingly.)
- ✓ Coming up with brand new ideas and new ways of doing/looking at things
- ✓ Writing based on your own personal experiences
- ✓ Talking about things that other people aren't talking about
- ✓ Using different media (infographics, video, audio, comics, whatever) to convey your information
- ✓ Being fiercely opinionated and justifying your opinions

While I do believe that creating great, unique content is the best way to get people to love you, there are other things you can do, too. Be yourself. Be a real person. No one wants to read blog posts from a robot. Write the way you speak, and let your personality shine through. Help people get to know you better through your content.

Final Words

One last thing. Give your audience permission and encouragement to engage with you. My favorite way of doing this is asking specific, direct questions at the ends of my blog posts. Give your readers plenty of reasons to interact with you.

Setting out to build an engaged community can seem like a daunting prospect, but it really isn't all that complicated. Sure, it takes time and hard work, but it isn't rocket science. Treat your readers well and they will treat you well. Love them and they will love you.

Remember, *all you need is love.*

Now I'm off to write a blog post dissecting the deeper meanings of *Yellow Submarine.*

Tristan Higbee (@trisanhigbee) is a traveler, adventurer, and proiific professional blogger.
<u>Start of Audience Building</u>: 2009
<u>Blogs and Websites</u>: TheBacklight.com, TristanHigbee.com, TheAloof.com
<u>Our Favorite Blog Post</u>: How to Guarantee 100 Comments on a Blog Post

Have You Told Anyone About This Book?

If you have, then thank you very much!

And if you haven't, and you like what you're reading, then would you mind helping to spread the word to others who might benefit from these ideas?

Like I wrote earlier, I'm not a big publishing company, and I don't have a big marketing budget, ties to the media, or relationships with booksellers. My entire marketing department is <u>you</u>.

So can you take a few minutes to help me spread the word? Here's what you could do:

- ✓ Tell your friends and loved ones about this book, or even buy them a copy.
- ✓ Visit the site, and use the buttons on the homepage to tweet, like and share the book to your networks.
- ✓ Go to Amazon.com, and write a review. This will really help us out!

I know that I can count on you, and knowing that really means a lot.

Thank you in advance for your help.

www.EngagementFromScratch.com

Section 3: Why and How to Do Content

So now you know your audience, and you're excited about creating content for them. But what to create? And how? That's the subject of this section…

The Blog Tyrant's post, "It's Like Starting a Riot in London", tells you that if you genuinely help people you'll win their loyal support.

Derek Halpern's essay, "Design+Format+Topic", teaches that how easy it can really be: position, create, promote, and connect – and you're done!

Onibalusi Dele's article, "If I had to start over…", shares his view that the most important things are to love, respect, and appreciate your readers.

Without further ado, let's get to it… why and how to do content in order to grow an engaged audience, from scratch.

The Blog Tyrant: It's like Starting a Riot in London

If you can genuinely help people, you'll win their loyal support.

Normally when I talk about growing an audience, I tell people to be themselves and solve problems and infuse their histories into everything that they write.

And while that is all good advice, it is only part of the solution.

If you take a deeper look at the way people behave, you will notice that there are certain emotional and psychological triggers that get people roused, mobilized and engaged.

Let's be clear. I am totally against rioting, theft or any other form of illegal behavior. That being said, the riots in London in mid-2011 provide a really striking example of what gets an audience ticking.

Missing Out On Something

Humans are wired to get motivated when they feel like they are going to miss out on something. It's a part of our behavior that dates back thousands and thousands of years to a time when food, water and shelter were more tricky to come by.

Marketing has known about this trigger for decades. Tell someone that they are going to get something for free and they get a little bit excited. Tell someone that there are only 10 left, and the phone rings off the hook.

People hate the thought of missing out on something.

That being said, you have to offer something that is worth wanting. People aren't going to go crazy over a used tissue box or some badly written eBook. They are, however, going to go crazy over a plasma TV that the next door neighbor just looted for free.

The psychological trigger of not missing out on something is very closely linked to the next point: feeling like part of an exclusive group.

86

Being Part of Something Exclusive

If you can convince someone that by being part of your audience they automatically become part of an exclusive club, you will go a long way to creating a loyal, active and long term fan.

Exclusivity is extremely important in garnering support and building an engaged audience. Take a look at any of the premium brands around the world and you will see what I mean.

People don't drive luxury cars because they are after a well-performing, economical car. They drive them because it makes them part of an exclusive club.

Don't get me wrong, luxury models are extremely well-built cars. But I would hazard a guess that if you put a mid-range brand name against a luxury model at the same price level, people would take the exclusive brand every time, regardless of the pros and cons.

Apple fans I've talked to are extremely loyal because they feel like they are part of an anti-PC club.

Both Apple and its PC counterparts make extremely good products, but only Apple has the religion-like following. There is a lot to be learned from their marketing and branding exercises such as the adverts that say, "If you don't have an iPhone, you don't have…"and then lists numerous amazing features.

People need to be part of a group. It is built into us. We get married and have kids and play sports and join clubs. Sometimes we start riots. And sometimes people join a riot even when they have no real reason to, just because they are so desperate to be part of a group.

If you want to grow an audience on a blog, or a website, or around a brand, you need to find a way to make people feel like they are part of an exclusive group. You can do it by offering limited rewards or by mobilizing around some specific cause. However you do it, people will be more likely to stick by you and your product if you can make them feel needed and special.

Making a Profit

As sad as it is, and as many problems as it has caused, one of the strongest psychological triggers for getting people engaged is to help them make more money. Like the previous two points, it is something that is wired into our very make-up.

Let's take a political example. In Australia there was a very successful Liberal Party Government that had run the economy extremely well, and kept Australians pretty wealthy for a long time.

However, in their second to last term, they ran into some ethical issues, specifically around joining the war in Iraq. The party was slipping in the polls, but come election time, they ran a campaign centered around the phrase, *"Who do you trust to keep interest rates low?"*

And they won the election.

People seemed to be more worried about their mortgages and their back pockets than they were about a war. The same is true of the London riots, and the same is true of growing an online audience. If you can help people pad their back pocket then you will get their loyal support.

Applying These Lessons to My Websites

I guess I should step back from the paper-thin metaphors and talk a little bit about how I apply this to my blogs and websites.

Let's use Blog Tyrant as a self-aggrandizing example. Here is a site in the overcrowded "blogging for profit" niche that got over 11,000 visitors in its third week, reached the front page of Delicious twice, and gets between 50 and 300 comments on every post. It is a great success, particularly considering the competition and the fact that 99% of the people who enter this niche end up failing.

So what did I do differently?

Well for starters, I wrote massively long posts (2,000+ words) that gave away huge amounts of information for free. And I only wrote them once a month, and closed comments after two weeks. This goes towards making the site feel exclusive, and making people feel like they are missing out on something if they don't stop by and leave a comment. Subscriber numbers started growing because people seemed to want to know when I published a post so they could leave a comment.

I then took things further by promising people that I would reply to every single comment I got. There's the group mentality. And to add to that mentality I constantly talked about working from home, playing tennis at lunch time and selling sites for $20,000 after just a few months. I wanted people to feel like they could achieve these goals and join this club by reading my posts.

I also wrote a bunch of hugely detailed and finger-numbingly long guest posts that "funneled" people back to my site's regular themes.

To elaborate: I created a free eBook about how to massively increase your email subscribers and then gave it away for free on my site. I then constantly wrote about how email subscribers are the key to working from home, playing tennis at lunch, etc. Finally, I went out and wrote really useful guest posts that touched on themes in my free eBook. This strategy worked as a "pre-sell"; getting people interested in my eBook before they even knew it existed.

Changing the Lives of Thousands of People

Quite literally, if you successfully grow an audience, you can change the lives of thousands of people. And if you set out to make yourself as valuable, informative and helpful as possible you will get that coveted following.

The things I have written above are just little tricks for making your valuable content appear more interesting. They are the salt on the chips.

Rather than starting riots your blog or website can create something much more powerful – a friendly community. When I feel alone, I know I have hundreds of followers that I can email for a chat. When I need to find a missing font, I can shoot a message off to Twitter and people will fall over themselves to find it for me.

I strongly believe that this love and affection comes about because I genuinely try to help my readers every time I put finger to keyboard. Make sure your content or product is helping people become happier, or don't even bother.

The Blog Tyrant (@BlogTyrant) is a mysterious blogger bent on taking over the blogosphere, and helping you to do the same.
Start of Audience Building: 2010
Blogs and Websites: BlogTyrant.com
Our Favorite Blog Post: How Do You Know When You're Cooked?

Derek Halpern: Design+Format+Topic

It's easy: Position, Create, Promote, Connect!

If you're looking to get more traffic to your blog, then pay close attention.

I'm Derek Halpern, the founder of SocialTriggers.com, and I've created wildly popular blogs in a variety of niches, including entertainment, fashion, makeup, marketing, and web development.

And when I say wildly popular, I mean wildly popular...

I'm not talking about a few hundred thousand hits here and there. To date, I've generated around 100 million hits across all of my sites.

How did I do it?

I developed a simple four-step process that works... GUARANTEED.

Hard to believe?

Maybe.

But I'm not asking you to believe anything just yet. I'm just asking you to refrain from disbelieving while I show you my proof, and my process.

So get ready to put some notes in the margins, and let's dive in.

Step 1: Position Your Blog in the Marketplace

Here's the deal:

If you plan on skipping this step, stop reading right now, because everything else will be pointless.

But if you're ready to take action, keep reading.

No matter what niche you're in, you need to provide people with a good – make that great – reason to visit your site, and an even better reason to keep coming back.

The truth is that the internet is getting crowded, and if you don't provide them with these reasons, you'll blend your way into obscurity.

A few years ago, merely creating *good content* was *good enough*. But now, with millions of blogs, many of which are stellar, content is no longer enough. Now you also need a *unique position in the marketplace*, or else you risk picking up what I call "traffic scraps," a.k.a. "I-get-no-traffic syndrome".

But don't worry – developing a unique position is much easier than you think, because *it's not about new ideas*. It's about my proven "Design+Format+Topic" blog differentiation formula.

#1. Content Design

The first, and easiest, way to make your blog unique is by having a unique design.

For example, if you find that most of your competitors run sites with blue or red links, use purple links. Or, if many of your competitors run magazine-style blogs, you can run a more traditional-style blog.

I know this sounds silly, but it's important, because it gives people something to remember you by. You're no longer just one blog in the crowd, you're that blog that people can easily picture in their minds.

How can you differentiate your design, without being a designer?

First, see the color schemes your competitors use, and figure out a color scheme for your site that is unlike theirs.

Then, pay attention to how they design their articles. Do they have images in their posts? How do they use them? Then figure out how you can do that differently too. For example, if they use stock photos, you can use stick figure drawings.

#2. Content Format

If you're looking to position your site, content format is almost as easy as choosing a unique design.

If your competitors run articles, you can run videos. If they run videos and articles, you can create PDFs or webinars.

You might not have a unique topic to write about, but if you deliver the content differently than anyone else, you'll attract people who enjoy that method of delivery.

For example, with my marketing blog, I started by offering webinars exclusively. At that time, webinars weren't really being used in the marketing blogosphere, so it helped me stand out and attract thousands of new email subscribers in just one month.

Now you're wondering what types of content exists? Here's a long, but not exhaustive, list of the different types of content that you can create to stand out from your competitors:

- ✓ Articles
- ✓ Videos
- ✓ Audio
- ✓ Teleseminars
- ✓ Webinars
- ✓ PDF reports
- ✓ Pre-recorded webinars
- ✓ Checklists
- ✓ Whitepapers
- ✓ Live streaming video
- ✓ Infographics

#3. Content Topic

Here's where things get a little more difficult.

If you're looking to create a blog with a huge audience, you need to come up with a newish niche topic.

With millions of blogs, it's hard to find a completely new topic, but you can simply combine 2 or 3 topics together to form a brand-new topic.

For example, when I launched Social Triggers, I decided to focus in on psychology research, conversion rate optimization, and then blogging and marketing.

These are not new topics individually, but when I combined them together, it was "newish".

You might be scared that you'll eliminate a lot of your audience by developing too specific a niche, and while that's possible, don't worry.

It's better to be known for something than to be known for nothing.

And once you develop your brand, and you're known for something specific, you can always branch out later.

For example, when Copyblogger launched, Brian Clark focused in on copywriting + blogging.

Once he built his brand on that, he branched out to other specialities like email marketing, search engine optimization, and content marketing.

Seem simple enough, right?

Right.

So remember to focus in on a specific combination of niches, and then branch out later.

And now we can move on to Step 2.

Step 2: Create Remarkable Content (it's easier than you think)

Seth Godin said it best. To create something remarkable, you need to create something worthy of remark.

Luckily, people tend to remark on the same exact things... no matter what niche you're in.

In the book Buzz Marketing by Mark Hughes, he talked about the six buttons of buzz, and when you create content that pushes one, two, or even three of those buttons, it's often worthy of remark.

What does that mean for you?

When you push those buttons, you'll find that people talk about your content on social media, blogs, and everywhere else you can imagine.

Sounds crazy, I know, but bear with me for a few seconds.

The six buttons of Buzz from Hughes are as follows:

1. Taboo
2. Unusual
3. Outrageous
4. Hilarious
5. Remarkable (really cool, or surprising)
6. Secrets (both kept and revealed)

To learn more about them, you should read Mark Hughes's book, but here's how this applies online right now:

No matter what content you create, you want to push one of these buttons, because these are the proven topics that people talk about.

For example, a few weeks ago I wrote an article called "The Content is King Myth Debunked."

I published it on my new marketing blog, and over the next few weeks, it received thousands of hits, hundreds of social media shares, and more than 100 comments.

The real benefit was this: Not only did it score me tons of links to my site, it also attracted LOADS of new subscribers into my email list...

...all because I pushed three buzz buttons. First, it was slightly outrageous, because marketers all say that "content is king" and I'm calling it a myth. It was also a little bit of taboo.

But most importantly, I talked about new research that I discovered, so I smashed the "secrets" button down hard, and the article really took off.

Step 3: Promote Your Content... The Smart Way

Once you've established your unique position, and created some remarkable content, it's time for you to get the word out.

The funny thing is that this is where most people mess up. They spend time creating content, and fail to promote it the right way.

How do you know if you're doing it right?

Let me put it like this. When you write an article, if the only promotion you do is to tweet, share on Facebook, and give it a +1, you're doing it wrong. Really wrong. Very wrong.

People who follow you on those networks are your fans, and yes, they have the potential to spread it to new people.

But the real growth comes from getting links on large websites that have never featured you before.

How do you get those links?

Simple: you ask them.

Here's what I do:

When I write an article, I think about my target audience. Once I know who that is, I find ways to reach that audience.

For example, when I wrote the article "The Content is King Myth Debunked," I knew that I was targeting three different audiences.

First, I was targeting the marketers, because I was talking about conversions. I was also targeting designers because I was citing research that showed the power of web design. And finally, I figured out that traditional writers would love this too because it "attacked" their precious craft.

I then went to Alltop.com, and found blogs that were related to those main audiences. Once I had a list of similar blogs, I emailed each of them a personalized pitch talking about the article I had written.

And guess what happened?

When you take the time to craft a personal email, and share something valuable with people, they respond... positively.

Go figure, right?

Send people valuable, interesting content, and they actually want to read it! :-)

So what happened?

Many of the people that I pitched either linked to me, or shared my article with their audience. That's how that article generated so much traffic and leads. I didn't wait for the traffic to come – I went out and found it!

And you can do the same.

As I said, decide who your target audience is, and go out there and cold pitch bloggers who might enjoy that article. You can find those bloggers on Alltop.com.

Step 4: Convert Your Traffic into Email Subscribers / Customers

If you look at your stats, you'll find that you get loads of new people to your site... most of whom visit, and never come back.

However, when you focus on turning these random visitors into loyal subscribers and customers, the growth of your site is often exponential.

For example, if you get 10,000 people to your site in March, and manage to keep 1,000 of them, then the following month, you can get another 10,000 people and you'll see that you hit 11,000 people for the month.

And if you do that for a year, you'll find that you've essentially doubled your traffic because your base will be at about 12,000 people.

How do you focus on retaining these new visitors?

Right now, in almost every niche that I know, you'd want to focus on converting people into email subscribers. Especially if you're writing articles that teach people how to do things.

(If you're running a news site, you should focus on emails still, but instead of sending out daily updates, create a curated news email letter that saves people time).

While conversion is often a dark and mysterious science, you can take advantage of 80% of the benefits by doing these three things:

1. Put email signup forms on your site in the right places.

You can create complex split tests, but who has time for that?

(I do because that's my business, but you? You probably just want to focus on creating the content that you love to create, right? Right.)

So where do you place the sign up forms? There are three key places, and they are:

1. At the top of your sidebar
2. At the end of your blog post

3. In your site's header (at the top of the page), or right below your site's header in a feature box (like on SocialTriggers.com)

2. Create an Incentive for people to sign up

Right now, incentives for emails is common-place. The reason why is because people are hesitant to part with their emails, and that incentive usually pushes them over the edge to subscribe.

What types of incentives can you use?

Personally, I'm a big fan of webinars as an incentive because they're high value and people love them.

You can also use PDF documents, audios, videos, and all that type of content, but that's what most people do nowadays which is why I prefer the webinars.

And as I said earlier, if you're running a news site primarily, the incentive could be something as simple as saving your readers time by summarizing the news for them.

3. Do nothing...

...because if you focused on step 1, and positioned your site so that it holds a unique spot in the market place, people will WANT to subscribe and hear from your site.

The Bottom Line

Is this the most exhaustive list of building websites that get TONS of traffic?

Likely not, but it has worked for me on every single site I have ever developed.

And the best part is this:

This strategy is timeless.

I used this same strategy back in 2006 when I was growing an entertainment site. I used it in 2007 when I grew fashion and makeup sites, and most recently I used this exact strategy to grow my marketing blog Social Triggers in a few short months.

To quickly rehash, here's the bulleted list of everything you need to do:

1. Position your site
2. Create remarkable content

3. Promote that content

4. Convert random visitors into loyal visitors.

And that's that.

Now get to work! :-)

Derek Halpern (@DerekHalpern) is an expert marketer and serial web entrepreneur. He uses the perfect blend of data driven marketing (conversion rates, academic research, and personal case studies) and content marketing to get traffic, attract customers, and sell products online.

Start of Audience Building: 2010

Blogs and Websites: SocialTriggers.com; DIYThemes.com/thesis/

Our Favorite Blog Post: "The Content is King" Myth Debunked

Onibalusi Bamidele: If I had to start over...

Love, respect and appreciate your readers.

I started my blog, YoungPrePro.com, 14 months ago, and over that time I went through **a lot** of trial and error while building an engaged community. Even though I experienced some small successes that confirmed that I was on the right path, I didn't experience any significant progress until after 8 months of pretty much constant hard work.

I know better now, and I've learned so much that I think I'd be able to build a successful blog twice as fast if I had to start again.

If I had to start my blogging journey all over again and wanted to build an engaged community, here are some things I would do differently:

I'd Be Clear about What I Was Blogging About

This is one great mistake that I made for a very long time, and I see a lot of bloggers making the same mistake every day. Far too many bloggers do nothing to position themselves as experts. The true secret to encouraging engagement on your blog is letting people see you as an expert, and people won't be able to do that if you're a jack of all trades who is master of none.

Instead of blogging about 5 different topics at the same time, you should analyze your blog and choose one specific topic you'd like to be known for. Choose a major niche and focus on covering just that, and other closely related topics. For example, if you want to write about online business, you could focus on the topics of blogging and building a successful blog – this way people will see you as an authority when it comes to blogging, and will happily interact with you as far as the subject is concerned.

Clarity is very important when it comes to building a successful blog. Choosing just one topic, and giving it your very best, will allow you to achieve far greater results, much faster than the average blogger.

I'd Have Started Guest Blogging Sooner

In my blogging career I have tried everything under the sun to generate traffic to my blog but have yet to see a tactic as effective as guest blogging. If I had to start from scratch I would start guest blogging from day one because even if I didn't have any content on my blog, I could still funnel that traffic to my mailing list.

Guest blogging is the most effective tactic you can use when trying to build a great blog because there are no restrictions on what you can achieve with it. Guest blogging can be easily used by anybody – new bloggers, and people who've been blogging for years. Just learn how to guest blog smartly and focus all your efforts on it.

The two main reasons why I guest blog nowadays is to get an instant boost in traffic and subscribers, and also to boost the search engine rankings of some of my most popular posts – guest blogging has been very effective in both situations.

Another thing I'd do as far as guest blogging is concerned is realize the importance of the Pareto Principle which states that 80% of the results you get come from 20% of your effort. This means instead of writing hundreds of guest posts for various blogs I will focus my efforts on writing only a few select guest posts for the top blogs in my niche. That's what I do now, and it is working fantastically.

One major thing that made guest blogging so effective for me and ensured that I got results faster than a lot of bloggers was that I put tons of effort into it. Instead of writing 2 or 3 guest posts in one month there were weeks when I challenged myself to write as many as 15 guest posts. When people started seeing my name on their favorite blogs repeatedly, they were much more likely to visit my blog and see what I had to say.

I'd Start Building My Email List from Day 1

This was my very worst blogging mistake, and I'm still regretting not starting an email list *on the very same day* that I started my blog. Every one of the most successful posts that I've written has resulted in new subscribers to my email list. And whenever I write a great post, the first thing I do is send it to my list: with the visits from all of the subscribers on my list, it is only a matter of time before the post goes viral.

The importance of building an email list should *never* be underestimated, because your email list is your #1 asset as a blogger. You should know that not all of your readers will subscribe; only your best readers, the ones who trust you, will subscribe, which is why the list is so valuable. The list gives you easy access to people who trust you and are committed to your success, and this will make it a lot easier for you to foster engagement on your blog – as opposed to waiting around for the next surge of traffic to come and bring with it a spike in reader engagement.

I'd Pay More Attention to My Readers

Respect is reciprocal. This means that if you visibly appreciate your readers' time by responding to their comments and queries, they will reciprocate with more comments, and by sharing your posts, because they will be that much more appreciative of the effort that you put into producing it.

Whenever someone reads and comments on a post of yours, take the time to give them a personal response – especially if they voice a question or concern. Make it clear that you love, respect and appreciate their part in making your blog a success, and they will keep on doing their best to help you reach and stay at the top.

Do all of this, and you will have an audience that truly loves you. And if your audience truly loves you, they will share that opinion every time you write a new post, and help you to spread the word.

Onibalusi Bamidele (@YoungPrePro) is a 17 year old internet marketer and blogger and the founder of YoungPrePro.com.
Start of Audience Building: 2010
Blogs and Websites: YoungPrePro.com
Our Favorite Blog Post: The 9 Challenges of a Freelance Writer

Section 4: Why and How to Do Social Media

After you start creating content for your fledgling audience, it's time to start spreading the word on social media, and empowering them to do the same.

Adam Toren's contribution, "Social Media from Scratch", explains that you should design your whole campaign around a two-way dialogue with your audience.

Gini Dietrich's essay, "Stroke People's Egos", teaches that you just need to stroke people's egos – it's really that simple.

Marcus Sheridan's article, "5 Levels of Networking Like a Superstar", shares his view that good networking is king, and awesome content sure does help!

Without further ado, let's get to it… why and how to do social media in order to grow an engaged audience, from scratch.

Adam Toren: Social Media from Scratch

Design your whole campaign around a two-way dialogue with your audience.

What would I do if I had to start my social media marketing all over today?

I would certainly do a lot of things differently than when we first started using social media for our businesses. What I've found over the past few years of managing our businesses' social media accounts is that there is definitely a right and a wrong way to go about using social media successfully. And starting out right from the beginning makes everything you do from that point forward much easier – and much more effective!

I always find it interesting that even though entrepreneurs recognize the importance of planning in nearly every aspect of their business, so many business owners dive into social media with hardly a thought about how they'll make it work for them. This is probably because it's so easy for anyone to create accounts on the various social media networks and just start posting. You don't have to learn much or be technically inclined, and it doesn't cost anything.

As with most of the entrepreneurs I know, we jumped into the social media scene without a real plan. We made the mistake of thinking that setting up accounts on Twitter and Facebook and posting links to the day's blog posts was enough to run successful social media campaigns. In reality, you can't even really call that a campaign. We did pick up quite a few followers, just because we have significant traffic on our websites, but in the beginning, we didn't really do anything that would create a community.

What is Social Media Good For?

What I've realized since first beginning to use social media is that the one thing social media is really good for is *connecting with your audience*. Building a community of engaged followers is invaluable to any business, and social media does that better than anything else I've seen. Unlike other forms of marketing, social media gives us the opportunity to have a two-way dialog with customers, and with potential customers. It provides an easy way for people to share their experiences with our businesses with their friends and connections, and it can give people the sense that they really 'know' your company.

All of that adds up to a tremendous opportunity for increased website traffic, and ultimately, raising your bottom line. The reason social media can have such a positive impact is that people who are part of your community, feel they know your business and are truly connected with you are much more likely to respond when asked to visit your website, or purchase your offerings. It's just common sense that the more of a connection someone feels with a company, the better they feel about using that company's products and services.

Building that connected, engaged community can be harder than it looks.

You might get a large number of followers without applying any social media marketing best practices, but it isn't the number that matters most. You can have thousands of Facebook 'likers' and Twitter followers, but what's important is how many of them actually care what you have to say. Those who feel they're members of your community are *interested* in your social media content. They look forward to your posts and often interact with you and/or share your content with their connections.

It's the number of *those* community members that will positively impact your bottom line.

So how do you build that community and reap the benefits of this powerful medium? How do you get people to engage with you and become community members, rather than just followers?

If I had to start over in social media, there are specific steps I would take to make sure I was maximizing my efforts to see the best results. I would take the time to learn the best ways to build an engaged community, and I'd treat social media marketing as a serious marketing tool, rather than a casual pastime.

I would follow the steps below from the start and make an impact right out of the gate!

Step 1: Plan it out!

As with any important part of your business, planning should be the first step in building an effective social media marketing effort.

When we first started promoting our sites, we did what most people do: we just started posting without really determining what our goals would be or the strategy we would use to reach those goals. If I was starting today, the first thing I'd do is to sit down and create a social media marketing plan. That plan would answer key questions about what I want to accomplish and how I plan to make it happen.

The rest of the steps below would all be part of that plan.

Step 2: Determine Your Target

You should already know who your target audience is. If not, determining your market is a vital part of your business in general, so get this part done ASAP.

However you market your business, you'll struggle to maximize your sales until you truly determine who your ideal customers are. Moreover, you really need to know as much as possible about this target market.

Where do they hang out? What do they like, and what do they dislike? What are they talking about? What problems or concerns are they voicing?

Knowing the answers to these questions will help you design a social media plan that speaks to the wants, needs, and concerns of the people who are most likely to want what you have to offer.

I've always made a point of developing a clear understanding of exactly who our target audience is in any business I've been involved in, because I know how important this knowledge is.

In the early days of our social media marketing though, we weren't necessarily keeping the demographics of our audience in mind as we built our networks. Early on, I made the mistake of focusing on numbers rather than the quality of the community we were building.

Once I began to take into consideration who we were trying to reach, we saw a lot of improvement in the level of engagement we experienced from our followers. They were naturally interested in our content, because they were the ones it was meant for.

Step 3: Decide Where to Focus Your Social Media Efforts

Facebook and Twitter are the 'big two' in social media (with Google+ quickly gaining ground), and most people know of LinkedIn as a good social network for professionals. But for many businesses, YouTube, Flickr, Foursquare, and other social networks can be important marketing tools as well.

Research where the leaders in your industry have a presence and decide – based on your answers to the previous step – where your *customers* can be found. You don't have to be everywhere, but you don't want to miss an opportunity to reach your audience where they gather most.

We still focus the vast majority of our efforts on Twitter and Facebook, and we're starting to delve into Google+. But I know that we could see even more results if we were to optimize our YouTube postings and really work that platform. YouTube is now the second most used search engine in the world, so it really shouldn't be ignored.

Deciding on which social media sites to use is a lot like picking radio stations to advertise on. You want to place your radio ads on the stations your customers listen to. Ignoring some of these platforms can be like failing to advertise on the all-sports station when your target is men who drink beer!

Step 4: Plan Your Content

The content that you post on social media is *very* important.

If you don't plan your content, you aren't likely to create anything capable of maximizing your results. A lot of what you'll post on social media is in response to other people's posts, but you also need to plan out the type of content that you will deliver to your community on a daily basis. Posts to third-party sites and strategically placed links to your own site need to be mapped out, as well, to reach your audience where and when they are most likely to see them – and respond.

Step 5: Plan Your Time

Social media doesn't have to dominate your life, but it does take a certain amount of time, and you're much more likely to stick with it and manage it well if you plan in advance for when and how long you'll work on social media each day.

In the early days of our social media marketing, our posting and interaction was somewhat sporadic. With all of the things that an entrepreneur has to do, it's easy to put social media off to "later", or forget about it entirely. If I had made a plan to spend a certain amount of time on social media, at a certain time of day each day, I would have ensured consistency in our social media presence, which would have made it more effective.

Step 6: Engage!

From what I've seen, I would say that the majority of businesses using social media are 'doing it wrong,' and the most common error is just posting links without any engagement – which is what this book is all about!

To build a relevant community of people who feel they know you and your company, you've got to talk to them!

You might be seen as a good resource by linking to quality content, but that's not enough to get people to feel as though they're part of your community. It isn't necessary to post your lunch plans every day or get too personal, but posting questions to your audience, answering questions they ask, thanking them and commenting on their comments, and re-posting their content all goes toward building relationships. In the end, that's really what social media is all about.

The more relationships you build, the stronger your community is. The stronger your community, the more social media will pay off in your business. Period.

So, what would I do differently if I had to start social media marketing from scratch? A lot!

The good news is that it's never too late to start over in social media. If you start today with a good plan and then implement that plan, you'll begin to see the results you're looking for.

One of the great things about all these platforms is that what you've done in the past gets buried pretty quickly. So don't fret over not getting it right up until now.

With social media marketing, we can all start from scratch without starting over!

Adam Toren (@theBizGuy, @BusinessGenius) is a serial entrepreneur, mentor, investor, and co-founded YoungEntrepreneur.com.
Start of Audience Building: 1999
Blogs and Websites: Blogtrepreneur.com; YoungEntrepreneur.com
Publications: Kidpreneurs; Small Business BIG Vision
Our Favorite Blog Post: What Self Confidence Can Mean to Your Business

Gini Dietrich: Stroke People's Egos

Stroke people's egos – it's really that simple.

Everyone always wants to know what the secret community-building sauce really is. Well, I'll tell you. It's actually pretty simple.

Stroke people's egos.

Seriously. That's it.

I know. I know. Every time I say that someone always exclaims, "But I'm not in business to make other people feel good about themselves. I have to generate sales."

Yep. You and me both.

But people buy from people they like and trust. And, if you spend time stroking the egos of those people you want to buy from you, they are that much more likely to do so.

Starting from Scratch

So let's start at the beginning.

Three years ago, I began blogging for the sole purpose of figuring it out so we could counsel clients on the pros, the cons, the whys, and the hows of making a blog effective.

And something interesting happened along the way. I built a community.

It wasn't on purpose. I had 128 visitors the first month of blogging. No one commented; not even my mom.

But I began reading other blogs, and commenting on them. Soon, those bloggers came to my blog and commented on my content.

Well, let's be real. It took me 10 months to figure that out. But when I figured that out, our traffic jumped, oh, nearly four thousand percent. Yes, *four thousand percent*.

110

All I was doing? Stroking other people's egos by commenting on their blogs and being smart about what I said.

The funny thing is that, when you comment consistently, the blogger wants to know who you are. So they check you out. And, if they like what they see, they comment, subscribe, and share.

Growing an Audience

But they have to have something to check out, right?

Yes, they do.

You have to have some really good content that makes them want to comment on, subscribe to, and share.

You'll hear different pieces of advice about your content. Mine is only to *be consistent*. There are daily newspapers, weekly newspapers, and monthly magazines. Decide which you want to be, set expectations, and deliver.

For instance, let's say you only want to blog once a week. Great! Which day is it going to be and by what time can I expect your content?

If you are consistent and people know what to expect, you'll succeed.

Back to building community. After I figured out the stroking egos part of content development, I realized I had to have some consistency.

So Tuesdays and Thursdays, by noon, were the expectations I set. And our traffic jumped 84 percent during the following year.

People were commenting, the blog was getting some notice, and things felt good.

Building Community

But, of course, for this double type A personality, that wasn't enough. I wanted more than just traffic and comments.

I wanted community.

I read a blog post that Mitch Joel wrote about community. He said (I'm paraphrasing) that you don't have a community until people begin talking to one another without your participation. Until then, it's just comments.

And he's right. You know you've hit community mecca when people come to your site to talk to one another, with your content as the conversation starter.

One of the things we did to really help build community was install Livefyre as our commenting platform. You see, it invites people to come back over and over and over again.

But it's not the end all, be all. It's only a tool. It's in how you use it that makes community building successful.

The consistent content has to drive conversation. For instance, on Fridays we do Gin and Topics, which are the top five pieces of content you should make you sure you don't miss. And, for the most part, most of it is fun and doesn't require a lot of thought.

Because of that, Friday afternoons on Spin Sucks is like attending a cocktail party. And it's FUN.

And then we get back to business on Monday morning.

Additional Things to Consider

So we've talked about stroking people's egos, having good and consistent content, creating a conversation, installing Livefyre, and providing some banter so it's not all serious all the time.

A few additional things you should consider:

1. Know what **your vision** is for the blog. It's easy to forget when you read other blogs and you're moved so much by what the bloggers have written that you want to write something similar. Unless it matches your vision, don't do it.

2. **Have goals**, just like you do for everything else you do in business. We started out with silly goals, such as "beat Danny Brown in the AdAge rankings," – which does a good job of keeping me motivated, but doesn't do much for the business. Know what you're trying to achieve and don't take your eye off the ball.

3. Your content should **always have a call-to-action** to it. This was a really hard lesson for me to learn. When I figured that out, this last year, our traffic

grew 281 percent. Our community grew. And you know what else? Our sales increased because we gave people a reason to buy from us.

Three years of blogging. Nearly a 30,000 percent increase in traffic since the beginning. Ten blog posts per week (four from guests). A highly engaged community. And increased sales.

Look ma, it works! It really works!

Gini Dietrich (@GiniDietrich) is the founder and chief executive officer of Arment Dietrich, Inc. and the founder of Spin Sucks Pro. She also is the author of Spin Sucks, the 2010 and 2011 Readers Choice Blog of the Year, a Top 42 Content Marketing Blog from Junta42, a top 10 social media blog from Social Media Examiner, and an AdAge Power 150 blog.
Started Audience Building: 2008
Websites and Blogs: SpinSucks.com; SpinSucksPro.com; ArmentDietrich.com
Our Favorite Blog Post: Your Mom Tells you What you Want to Hear

Marcus Sheridan: 5 Levels of Networking Like a Superstar

Great networking is king, and awesome content sure does help!

I wasted a year of my blog's life simply because I had no clue how to network and build a community.

That's right – 1 Year… 52 Weeks… 365 Days… call it what you want, but it seemed like a long dang time.

Despite writing what was pretty decent content 3-4 times a week, I was essentially a billboard in the desert – great to see but no eyes to see it. Frustrating? Heck yeah it was.

But this all changed when I stopped listening to the *'Content is King'* talk and applied myself more to the idea that *'Great Networking is King and Awesome Content Sure Does Help'*.

So that's what this little article is all about.

It's meant to take you on a trip that will, if done properly, expand your online community beyond anything you've dreamed possible. And because I've applied the things I discuss in this article, my blog today is one of the strongest communities on the web. The number of comments, personal emails, and discussion I get with each new post is truly mind-boggling and humbling as well.

If you want to be a star online, here's how to network like one, and hopefully it won't take you a year to figure this out as it did me. ;-)

So let's go through all 5 levels of essential networking online…

Level I: Comments/RT 101

Ahh yes, you're just getting into the world of blogging and doing everything you can to learn the ins and outs. After producing your first bit of content and realizing no one is looking at your stuff, as well as the fact that Google couldn't care less about you, you decide that maybe **networking is the answer**.

Knowing this, you read on other blogs about the power of commenting and so your off to the races…and you commence the process of finding blogs and leaving your typical "Great post! Well done! You rock!" comments.

It is also during this time that you find out about Twitter and this odd thing called 'retweeting'. Now, while you're reading the articles and leaving your quick comments, you hit that little green button and RT the post. Not being sure what to say or how to say it, you don't really add anything to the tweet but hey, it's a start, and you're beginning to make it happen… and you've commenced Level I.

Level II: Advanced Commenting and RT

Now that you've been going the standard commenting and RT route for a while, you realize that maybe your comments and RTs aren't as effective as they could be. You notice other bloggers leaving incredibly thoughtful comments on various blogs you read. You also pick up on Twitter pros that not only retweet, but also make the tweet so appealing that you've just got to look behind the curtain.

After seeing so many great examples, you think to yourself, "Hey, just by adding some depth and creativity to my comments and tweets, I bet I can get much better results." And so there you go. Your comments are now great. Your RTs are appealing and insightful. You've now entered Level II.

Level III: Learning to Give Love

Now that you've mastered the art of thoughtful commenting and retweeting, you're ready for your next challenge.

After further study, you start to notice a pattern of the higher level bloggers: they have a tendency to mention others.

In fact, with a deeper look, you start to see a definitive pattern in that most of the top bloggers spend as much time talking about others as they do themselves. You notice how these folks have this masterful way of mentioning others throughout their writings. In fact, now that you've spotted the pattern, you see it more and more and more from all the upper-level bloggers.

So you give it a try.

And immediately you notice two things – you feel great for helping others and your relationships with those persons grow stronger and stronger as everybody wins. Life is getting good and you're now a Level III networker.

Level IV: A Complete Focus on Promoting Others as Much as Yourself

Now that you've established the pattern of looking to mention the good deeds of others within your blog posts you find that your network has grown tremendously from the time you started to the point where you now are. It feels good to be surrounded by great people and not only is your blog growing nicely because of these relationships, but you also find yourself genuinely caring for the success of other. You don't just want them to succeed; you *really* want them to succeed.

This is when you decide write full-blown articles, expecting nothing in return, about people or products you feel are changing the world. And as you do this, your relationships and network reach a new level of strength and synergy. You've found your inner circle, and you're now a Level IV networker.

Level V: Above and Beyond

You've arrived.

You're now running a hugely popular blog with an army of supporters and fans at your side. It feels great and each day with it brings more passion, excitement, and energy. But now that you've reached this point, you're looking for different ways to give back and go above and beyond to show kindness to others while building your networking community.

Let me give you the perfect example of a Level V behavior, as they're tougher to describe. I recently commented to **Ingrid** at NittyGriddy blog that I was still very new with Twitter and working hard to understand the entire culture and how to make the medium work effectively for me. Knowing this, Ingrid emailed me and asked me for my shipping address. I happily gave it to her and a few days later I got a package in the mail from Amazon, with a book inside called, '**The Tao of Twitter**', written by the social media thought leader **Mark Schaefer**. As you might imagine, when I received this book I was floored by Ingrid's above and beyond thoughtfulness. This, my friends, is a Level V networking at its finest.

So there you have it folks, 5 levels of networking that will take your online community to levels you never dreamed possible. I want to point out also that this is not an exact science, and when I offer these levels, I'm speaking completely in general terms.

To close, I'd like to offer this one critical piece of advice and if you follow it and nothing else I've mentioned here, I know you're going to be very successful.

Before every blog article you ever write, ask yourself this simple question:

Who can I help today with this article?

If you truly ask this question, and then follow the promptings that come your way, readers will see just how important community is to you and will thus want to be a part of your special movement.

Marcus Sheridan (@TheSalesLion) is a master salesman, author, active blogger and niche marketing expert who used content marketing to grow his pool business into a national leader in the field, and blogs about how others can do the same.
Start of Audience Building: 2009
Books and Publications: Stop the Yawns; Teen Talks to Stop the Yawns...
Blogs and Websites: TheSalesLion.com; RiverPoolsandSpas.com
Our Favorite Blog Post: 9 Lessons I Learned From the Biggest Blogging Jerk Ever

Have you got the FREE bonuses yet?

Sometimes we all need a little reminder – especially when we're busy doing lots of other things, and we're engrossed in a captivating book about audience building that we just can't put down. ;)

But seriously, have you got the free goodie bag yet? Here's everything that's included inside it:

- ✓ Detailed infographics clearly laying out the entire process taught in the book
- ✓ Worksheets to help you do everything that is discussed in the book, and do it well
- ✓ Templates that you can use to approach bloggers and build relationships
- ✓ Access to exclusive teleseminars, webinars, and coaching calls
- ✓ And a whole bunch of other cool stuff...

And remember, it's all 100% free for Engagement from Scratch! readers – that's you! Does that sound awesome or what? Go get it now:

bit.ly/efs-bonus

Section 5: Be Your Passionate Self

In the process of building your audience, you must never forget that you stand at the core of it all, and the only way that is right for you to build your audience is the way that is right for you.

Corbett Barr's contribution, "The Fear of Engagement", explains that yes, blogging and building an audience is hard – but you should do it anyway.

Evan Carmichael's post, "The Internet Helps Those Who Help Others", tells you that you should be yourself – honestly, and all the time.

Sean Platt's essay, "Grow the Right Audience", teaches that you just need to be yourself, write what you'd want to read, and talk to your audience.

Without further ado, let's get to it… why and how to be your passionate self in order to grow an engaged audience, from scratch.

Corbett Barr: The Fear of Engagement

Yes, blogging and building an audience is hard.
Do it anyway.

Here's a question you'll have to ask yourself if you plan to build a popular website: can you build a thriving, dedicated, engaged audience?

Can you?

Yes, or no?

What's it going to be?

Because it's not enough to build an audience. You need a *thriving* audience to create something really special.

I'm assuming that your answer is yes, that you think you can build a thriving and engaged audience. That's why you're reading this book, after all.

And since your answer is at least a qualified yes, you probably already know what you need to be doing to build that audience for your website. Don't you?

You know that you need to be creating amazing content and sharing it. You know that you need to be responsive to your audience and their needs. You know that you have to prioritize your tasks and manage your time well. You know that you need to be active in the communities that pertain to your industry. You know it all.

So why aren't you doing it? (Or why isn't it working?)

If you're at all like I was when I started blogging, you aren't out there engaging with your audience yet, because doing what needs to be done is daunting:

- ✓ It can take forever,
- ✓ Rewards, if they come, could come very slowly,
- ✓ You may have to disclose more about yourself than you're comfortable with,
- ✓ People will judge you,
- ✓ There's a ridiculous amount of competition,

✓ And, failure is a very real possibility.

These are all good reasons to be hesitant about getting out there and doing it, but none of them is a good enough reason not to get over it, and do it anyway.

Let's go through them, and see if there aren't some ways they can be worked around.

It Can Take Forever

I'm taking it as a given that you intend to create amazing, valuable, epic content. No one sets out to build an audience with the intention of creating mediocre or bad work, but few realize how much time it actually takes to create epic content. I know bloggers who spend upwards of 10 hours on a single post!

You may not need to spend that long to create content that is unique, inspirational and important, but you probably can't whip up a post that does all that in an hour.

And you may not have the experience or tools that you need to create epic content at all right now. Some people need months of learning and experimentation before they're equipped to create the level of insanely useful content that it takes to really stand out.

Once you have created your epic content, you need to promote it. Getting consistent traffic is a whole other subject, but you have to at least spend considerable time on social media sites and on developing relationships with other bloggers. Rome wasn't built in a day, and a thriving audience isn't built in a month.

Rewards Come Very Slowly

Except for those very rare occurrences of massive success from day one, it can take weeks, months, even years to develop an audience that you have a real connection with. Knowing that before you start out is intimidating at best.

You need to devote a ton of time to writing content, getting involved, getting to know your readers, and sharing your work. Eventually, if your content is as good as you know it is, it will start to pay off, and your audience will start doing some of that work for you.

Readers independently sharing your work doesn't let you off the hook, of course – you still need to write, promote and engage – but you'll start to see some return on your investment in the form of subscribers, and maybe even customers.

Hang in there. You'll make it.

You May Have to Disclose More Than You're Comfortable With

When I started blogging, I knew that I was going to be writing about and sharing my personal experiences and thoughts, but I never thought that I'd be in a situation where I was sharing personal details about me and my life with the whole wide web.

There came a point, though, when it was the best thing to do.

I was asking my readers to connect and empathize with me, and to make that a real possibility, I had to give them a reason. Eventually I wrote a post called "33 Things I've Never Told You (or, How to Re-Introduce Yourself and Kick Your Watered-Down Self in the Ass)", which garnered some of the most genuine responses and sharing I've ever had from my audience, and spurred dozens of other bloggers to do the same type of post, or something similar.

This taught me that in order to really engage with your audience, sometimes it's best to let them know who you really are.

It wasn't easy. It was one of those posts that I was a little afraid to publish, because it would expose me in an entirely new way to the public. It turned out to be one of the most important things I've ever written.

People Will Judge You

Welcome to the internet, land of a million critics.

If you're going to be putting yourself out there in a genuine way, then some people are going to judge you, and it's going to hurt if you let it. Sometimes negative feedback can be a great thing – it can point out the things that you could be doing better, and change the way you think about your own work and opinions. Other times, it will feel nasty and pointless – because that's exactly what it will be.

There are always going to be people who take pleasure or pride in bringing someone else down. These are "trolls", and no blog or forum is complete without them. Take comfort in the fact that if the Dalai Lama wrote a blog post, they'd be saying the same thing.

But it's not really trolls that we worry about.

It's the real people – the people who, up to this point, have read and enjoyed your content, and have made a connection with you, but who now, for some reason, have taken offense and called you out on it. Sometimes it can be someone you have a real relationship with. It's scary, and can be painful.

This is a risk that you have to take. It's all part of the growth process, and you'll learn what you're comfortable with and what you're not. Eventually you'll learn that if you try to please everyone, your content probably won't be worth reading.

There's a Ridiculous Amount of Competition

I've got a blog. My friends have blogs. Some of my family members have blogs. You have a blog. When someone opens a web browser, there are countless choices for them. Virtually every topic is blogged about, and most topics have many, many blogs. Getting someone to choose *your* site over all of the other options isn't easy.

This comes back to content, of course, and it also comes back to being patient and putting in your time. The more you write, and promote, and connect, the better you will be at all three. Being awesome at one of those three is okay, but being great at all three is what will really put you ahead of the curve.

Also remember that you're not always going to be the first choice for every web surfer out there. You just need to be the best about your topic for your particular niche. Cut down on the competition by competing in a smaller, less crowded market.

Ask yourself this question: "why should someone read *my* blog vs. the hundreds (or thousands) of other choices out there?" If you don't have a solid answer, it's time to re-evaluate what you're doing.

Failure is a Real Possibility

Plenty of blogs fail. In fact, most of them do. There's a new blog started every few minutes, and most of them never get more than a handful of readers – let alone any financial success.

So how can you avoid failure for your blog?

It will depend largely on what you decide to write about from day one. You need to make sure that the topic is both something that you're passionate about and something that other people will be interested in reading. This is not always as easy as it sounds, thanks in no small part to the above-mentioned competition.

It's important to remember that you, with your unique perspective, bring something valuable to the table. Your fear of failure, as valid as it may be, is only a sign that you're doing something challenging, pushing your own boundaries. Don't let it stop you from trying.

If you try to build an audience, you might fail. But if you don't try, you already have.

Once you take the plunge, and work your way through the initial obstacles, you'll find that you have an audience that listens to you and cares about what you say. They will let you know what they need from you, and engaging with them will bring you great satisfaction. One of the best feelings I've ever had has been to watch my audience grow, and hear from people that I've been able to influence in some small way.

At the end of the day, the only thing keeping you from creating your business, making your blog successful, and living the life you want *is you*. That doesn't mean that changing your mindset and overcoming all of the fears surrounding growing an audience isn't difficult – it just means that you *can*.

Corbett Barr (@CorbettBarr, @ThinkTraffic) is a prolific blogger and serial entrepreneur who writes about living the life you want and making your online ventures successful.
<u>Start of Audience Building</u>: 2010
<u>Blogs and Websites</u>: ThinkTraffic.com; CorbettBarr.com
<u>Our Favorite Blog Post</u>: Write Epic Shit

Evan Carmichael: The Internet Helps Those Who Help Others

Be yourself – honestly and all the time.

So how did I get into blogging?

I started doing business at the tender age of five, selling pictures door to door. From then until the age of 19, there was plenty of time for trial and error before joining a biotech start-up. We were successful, got acquired, and I ended up working with a venture capital company, raising millions of dollars in start-up capital for growth companies in Ontario, Canada. Because of my success with the biotech start-up, I was asked to speak at various events, and as a means of letting people know where I was going to be and when, I started EvanCarmichael.com.

And then I started getting readers.

Not just people looking for my next gig, but entrepreneurs asking me questions, seeking advice and looking for information. I started providing it, beginning mainly with the financing information that was my specialty. Eventually, I decided it was time to make the site profitable – I started asking other bloggers and authors to contribute content, and I started selling advertising.

It was a long, mostly unplanned journey from selling hand-drawn pictures door-to-door to running the influential entrepreneurship blog that I do today – and if I'd know where I was going in the beginning, I like to think I would have made it here a whole lot faster. You, reader, are lucky, because so many people have gotten to a comfortable level of success in the past, and are more than happy to share with you the things that worked, the things that didn't, and tons of other advice that you can use to drastically shorten your own journey to the top of your field.

EvanCarmichael.com makes all of its revenue from advertising; we don't sell a product or service, so some of the advice that I have to offer may not be completely applicable to your business model, but at least some of it will be, and I hope that after you finish reading this book, you'll come over and take a look at what we're doing.

Now, for the good stuff: building your audience.

No matter what your niche or area of expertise is, if you're starting from scratch, what you're going to want is reader engagement. A giant website with a readership in the millions can rely on advertising to generate enough income, but for a new blogger, quality is going to be much more important than quantity. How can you get this engagement? I'm going to share with you the five strategies that I use on EvanCarmichael.com to drive huge, engaged readership.

1. Create Fantastic Content, and Use Video

There is already a wealth of information out there about why and how to create great content, so I will only add here that creating amazing content will be easy if you are genuinely passionate about what you are doing. You can't fake it, and if you don't have that passion, eventually the work will become drudgery, your quality will drop and you will probably quit.

I would, however, like to add a comment about videos. I love videos, and so do blog readers. Creating a video can be time consuming, technically difficult, and sometimes expensive, but if it's within your power, I urge you to create one – or several!

Video will pay for itself over time – focus on a topic in your niche, maybe one that people frequently ask you questions about. Place it on your blog as a response to readers, and also email it to your newsletter list, put it on YouTube and other video sharing sites, submit it to directories and forums – basically use it to drive traffic back to your blog forever.

The point being: make videos.

2. Create Awareness with Social Media and Partnerships

Start with social media.

Find bloggers who have active, engaged Twitter feeds and follow them. Retweet their posts, send them information that is relevant to their niche, and eventually they'll take an interest in you, share your content, and help drive visitors to your site.

Create a LinkedIn profile and interact with people that way. Use Facebook and YouTube to share your content. In short, take advantage of any method that you can to engage with people.

Now that you've got great content, you need to get it out there. One way I like to do so is by partnering with other bloggers.

Request content from bloggers you love – many will be happy to write a guest post to you, and will likely direct their regular readers to your site to see it once it's published. On EvanCarmichael.com, we have content from over 6000 different authors. Having that many different viewpoints is an invaluable resource for my business. You don't need 6000 people writing for you to have the same effect, though – start with a few, and as your readerships grows, and your needs change, you can bring in more and more people.

Every month, we create a list of the 50 best blogs in a particular niche.

Contact every blogger on that list and let them know that they've made the cut. Very like, they will tweet about it, share it, and at the very least, come check out what it is you're doing. You can even create a little badge saying: "I was featured on So-and-So's best 50 list" that they can put on their own website. These are great because they're a great value for your readers, a great way to connect with other bloggers and very shareable.

3. Foster Familiarity with Photos

Familiarity is created by putting yourself out there. That means telling people your name, putting up some photos, and talking about yourself. Personal details will allow new readers to feel like they know you, and people like to do business (and buy from) people they know.

Initially, I didn't have pictures of myself on EvanCarmichael.com, even though the site was named after me. I figured: "Who am I? Why would anyone want to see my face, or know anything about me?" What I found though, was that people would very frequently ask who I was. The disconnect between my name on the website, and no information about who I was or what I was doing confused people.

You can avoid this mistake by identifying yourself to your audience. It comes down to building a personal, as well as a professional brand. Personal is always going to be easier, so if you can mesh the two, you'll find recognition and engagement much easier. It doesn't matter if you work out of a penthouse office or your basement – some pictures and personal details about yourself will show that you're a nice guy to work with.

One technique that I love to use is newsletters. I have a specific newsletter list, separate from my RSS feed, and I offer incentives for people to join. I always start off a newsletter with a little information about what I'm up to. Like the pictures on my site, and my introduction video, it's a way for people to connect with me on a personal level, even though I have no idea who they are. Little tidbits like: "I love baseball," or "I'm travelling to Boston this weekend," provide touch points that readers can relate to, and a reader that relates to you is a reader who will be loyal to you.

4. Position yourself as an Expert

Are you familiar with the name Mark Saltzberg? If you go to the movies in Canada, during the previews you're very likely to see Mark talking about some new gadget or gizmo. Mark wants to become *the* Canadian expert on technology, and doing these movie-preview spots has led to a host of opportunities for him – from television interviews,   to speaking engagements, to print interviews. Because he blogs as well, he's easy for people to find and connect with which – in the future this could lead to sponsorship deals, or a consulting business.

You may not be able to get yourself into previews at the movies, but there's no reason why you shouldn't come to be regarded as an expert in your niche. You've already got content that demonstrates your knowledge and ability, now you need to get people to start drawing on your skills. I recently signed up for a service called PRLeads.com. For about $99 a month, you have access to network of journalists looking for experts. These journalist post what they're currently writing about and you can present yourself to them as a resource. Doing this has gotten me into the New York Times and other huge, credible news sources.

When a new visitor comes to your blog and sees the organizations you've provided information to, it enhances your credibility and the perceived value of what you offer. That's a pretty good deal for $99 a month!

5. Help People

Helping people is one of the most enjoyable and satisfying aspects of being a blogger.

I help people solve business problems on my website, through email, and over the phone – however I can. I've got a large site with a large readership, so people come to me. You probably won't have that when you're just starting out – you'll have to go out and find people to help.

Within your niche, forums can be a good place to start, and a search for your keywords on Twitter will reveal many more people with questions you could ever answer!

If you can, connect with people via email or over the phone – the more personal you can get, the more likely it is that that person will become an engaged member of your audience, and share your content with their own network as well.

At the end of the day who you are as a person and a blogger is going to have a huge impact on how big your audience grows, and how engaged they are with you. Be sincere, be passionate and be personal.

Evan Carmichael (@EvanCarmichael) has been an entrepreneur since the age of five, when he and his sister sold drawings door to door. Now his blog helps thousands of entrepreneurs every month come closer to reaching their goals.
Started Audience Building: 2003
Websites and Blogs: EvanCarmichael.com

Sean Platt: Grow the Right Audience

Be yourself, write what you'd want to read, and talk to your audience.

Growing my first online audience was easy. But growing the *right audience* was one of the most difficult things I've ever done.

Once upon a time, I believed that getting attention was everything. If I gathered enough attention, I'd be able to easily convert it to currency, and quickly write my own "happily ever after."

But that's not the way it works – not online, and not anywhere else. Attention is just a trunk full of groceries. You still have to chop the ingredients, mix the sauce, toss the salad, and know exactly who's coming to dinner.

Get this wrong, and even if you have an eager table of diners shoving food in their mouths, they might not stick around for drinks. Or come to your next dinner.

Meeting People Is Easy

Gathering a crowd was easy. I poured my soul into everything I wrote, and did it on every day ending in Y. I made sure that when I published each day's 500 or so words, they would be good enough to stand tall and proud, even if they were the last I ever published.

I did everything right when it came to the quality of my content, but I was 100% wrong believing that was all that mattered. Because if you don't know *who* you're speaking to, you're not really speaking to anyone – even if the room is packed with people.

As an example, imagine that your goal is to sell women's shoes, but you're writing about power tools. Sure, you might reach a few husbands in the audience that are brave enough to buy their wife a pair of shoes, or maybe you'll be lucky enough to count a few female construction workers and maybe even a cross-dresser

132

or two among your audience, but the numbers are gonna be small if you're not actually writing about women's shoes.

Find Your Audience

To effectively engage an audience, and keep them around for the long haul, you have to be sure that you're writing to the right people. That means you must first determine your niche, and then write with specificity so you're entering the conversation that's *already taking place* in your reader's minds. The more narrow your niche and the less others are writing about it, the more you will stand out.

In an ideal world, you will be writing about your passion. The words will come easier and the copy you write will ring with the clarity of your true voice. If you love women's shoes, chances are great you can find excellent topics about women's shoes that will help you create some killer content.

The less research you have to do and the more natural knowledge and insatiable curiosity you have about a niche that you can bring to the surface of your copy, the better your work will be.

Once you have a general idea of what you'd like to write about, search the web to see what people are saying about your topic. Searching Google for a subject, along with the word "forum", will net you plenty of results. You can also find some of the more popular books on Amazon with lots of reviews. Pay attention to what's selling, and the language that people are using to talk about things.

This knowledge is incredibly powerful. Observing the language used in forums and reviews allows you to be a fly on the wall. Every conversation that you observe makes you more of an expert. Not only are posters and reviewers discussing the exact problems that their market is most concerned about, they're using the precise language of that unique environment.

Understand your market's language, and the ideas that drive it and you will be able to speak to them far more effectively. That will increase the conversions on everything you write, whether that means a comment, a re-tweet, or clicking a BUY button.

Don't Be Afraid of SEO

Showing up high in search engine results can make the difference between blogging in anonymity and being recognized as the authority that you're working so hard to become.

Search Engine Optimization is one of those terms that a lot of people hear, use, and throw around, but few truly understand. And while there is a science to it, it's not nearly the esoteric wisdom that some "SEO Ninjas" (people who want you to pay them a lot to "optimize your website") make it out to be.

If you understand that Google follows people and that people follow quality content, you'll already be ahead of many SEOs and future proof your content at the same time. Semantic indexing means that content written for people – rather than search engine bots – will continue to rise to the top of the search results, forever.

Use WordPress with basic SEO common sense and well written copy, and you'll have an SEO cocktail that will outperform much of your competition.

Engage, Engage, Engage!

I've learned to place intention behind my momentum, so that I'm not only moving, but moving consistently forward – in the best possible direction, and always toward where I ultimately want to go. The online landscape has changed tremendously since I started my online adventure three years ago.

If I were starting today, I would be smart enough to know that it's not the size of your audience that matters, but how engaged they are, and how much they've bonded to who you are and what you do.

Engagement is everything when it comes to social media. You get what you give. Always.

Marketing is made easy, or at least a whole lot easier than most people make it out to be, by building an audience that will be evangelical with your message, and do the heavy lifting for you. That won't happen unless you gather a crowd that is in alignment with your goals.

If your audience is responding – commenting, liking your posts on Facebook, re-tweeting you on Twitter, linking to your work in their own blog posts, or in any way helping spread your word – they are engaged.

But if your audience isn't responding, you're wasting time with every word you write.

Tell Stories

People love to hear a good story. Connect with readers by opening up and sharing parts of yourself in your blog posts. Just like you would in a friendship. *Of course, you might want to keep some of the more intimate details of your life out of your copy!*

The first thing to do when you're telling a story is to not address a mass of "readers", but rather treat your reader as an individual. You like when people talk to you directly, don't you?

You see what I did there, right?

And again, right there!

Treat your readers (or reader if you're going to narrow it down to the one reader you are writing to) like a friend. Be your most charming, best, wittiest self. And be conversational. Use this not only for your posting style, but also when you're telling your story.

One of the most important things you'll need to do is *remember to be authentic*. Most people can smell a phony a mile away, even over broadband. And the more salesy your content is, the more powerful this uncanny ability becomes. Marketing speak is not audience friendly, unless you audience is made up of marketers.

You must always be yourself. Don't manufacture stories, or exploit friends or family for post material (unless they're cool with that), and never tell a story that has no value to your audience, simply as a Trojan horse to sell something.

It's okay if your story *does help you sell something*, of course. But there must be value in the *story itself*. A good story must entertain, provoke thought, inspire, prompt change, spark debate or conversation, or make people feel a little less alone.

Ideally, your story will put your readers in the right frame of mind to respond to your Call To Action.

Act Now!

Your Call To Action is just the thing that you want your reader to do.

You're never writing just because – or at least, you shouldn't be. You might want them to buy something, but you might also want your reader to comment, or, more likely, simply share your content so that it gets out to other people, and helps you build your audience.

A good story can create kinship with others. A *great* story will get them to fulfill the Call To Action.

There's nothing greater than seeing people on Twitter, Facebook, and Google+ talking about you, telling people that they *must* check out a post.

It's even better when these same people are buying your product, paying for your services, or somehow helping your business to thrive. But that will never happen if people don't get to know you, and learn why you're different than everyone else on the Web.

Be Yourself

Be personal, but be pointed. Use the best of you to lead your audience where you want them to go, but make sure that *you know* where that is, and *what your purpose is* when you get there.

Take the time to do things right. Listen to your audience, so that you can become an asset in their lives. That's the best way, by far, to grow a high-quality, loyal base of followers. Once you establish trust and rapport, you will rarely if ever have to ask for likes and re-tweets – your audience will do it for you because they appreciate who you are, what you do, and where you're going.

It starts with attention, so grab as much as you can. But don't stop there. Actively nurture all the attention you get, turn it into engagement, and use that engagement to build the best business that you possibly can.

Pay Attention

Just as your readers will inform your content, they can also help you see when you've gone off the rails, or when trends have radically changed.

If your audience is suddenly responding negatively, or not at all, it could mean that you've lost touch. Keep in mind that as you get more popular, you *will get* more haters. It's just the way things are on the Web, and in real life.

So don't mistake an increase in haters as a sign you're doing something wrong, so long as they are still a minority of your overall readers. But if your readership is decreasing and criticism is *increasing*, you probably aren't writing to the right crowd.

Or maybe tastes have changed. Either way, you have a job to do.

People are fickle. You must stay on top of what's relevant in your niche. It doesn't mean that you have to agree with the common consensus – you should always stay true to who you are so you can guide your readers in the best possible direction. Be contrary if you feel genuinely contrary. But you need to know where people stand on an issue if you're going to write about it with knowledge or authority.

Sometimes, it's good to go against the trends. Especially when the trends are bad.

When a lot of bloggers started writing SEO content for search engines rather than humans, I ignored the trend. It didn't feel right to write for robots. Sure, you might get people to your website, but once there, they're going to leave if your content is keyword driven drivel. So I experimented, trying to find a happy medium to utilize keywords, but only in a natural way which would still be of value to readers.

Be a Friend, Gain a Friend

Blogging is a lot like being a friend. Or good acquaintance – the kind of person you enjoy being around, but don't have to commit a whole lot of time to (or help them move a couch on the weekend).

ENGAGEMENT FROM SCRATCH!

Be entertaining, be interesting, and always treat your readers with respect.

Be yourself, write stuff you're interested and you'd want to read, and talk to your audience. You'll be well on your way to mastering the type of engagement that matters most.

Sean Platt (@SeanPlatt) is a freelance writer, ghost writer, father, and prolific author of many popular books.
Start of Audience Building: 2009
Books and Publications: Writing Online, , How to Write a Sales Letter that Works, Yesterday's Gone, and manyothers
Blogs and Websites: GhostwriterDad.com; CollectiveInkwell.com
Our Favorite Blog Post: How I Stopped Being Stupid and Started Making Money as a Writer

Section 6: Stories and Lessons Learned

Now you've got all the building blocks, but it's always so much easier to learn from the stories and experiences of others who have done the same. That's what this section is about – case studies and lessons learned by four of our co-authors about how to build an audience, and how they built theirs.

Kristi Hines's contribution, "Three Wishes", explains that you must choose your brand carefully, create lists from day one, and be careful who you get involved with.

Linda Bustos's post, "Make Yourself Indispensable", shares her experience that you must make yourself absolutely and completely indispensable through purpose, differentiation, and flexibility.

Natalie Sisson's essay, "The Power of One", teaches that you must give, and give, and give, and give some more.

Steve Kamb's article, "One Email at a Time", shows you that audiences are built one fan at a time.

Without further ado, let's get to it... the stories and lessons learned by these audience builders in their process of growing an engaged audience, from scratch.

Kristi Hines: Three Wishes

Choose your brand carefully, create lists from day one, and be careful who you get involved with.

Now that I'm on the brink of turning my blog into a business, I can look back on my blogging career and be satisfied with how I've done things. If I had to start over, however, there are three areas I would approach differently.

Branding Your Name Matters

If I could begin again, I would use my name as my brand from day one. If there was only one thing I could go back and change, or a genie could grant me just one wish, this would be what I would choose.

Whenever you meet someone, you introduce yourself by name. When you RSVP for an event, you do so with your name. There are myriad occasions when your name will be what people see first.

When I started out blogging, I branded myself as Kikolani for my blog. I setup profiles on forums and social networks with the username @kikolani. Everything was Kikolani. I've always loved the name, but using it did cause branding complications that didn't surface until several months down the road.

It started with friend requests on Facebook. I would add someone as a friend, and they would accept. Then a few weeks or months later, I would receive a post on my wall or a private message that said something to the affect of: "OH, you're KIKOLANI!" This happened again on my LinkedIn profile, because on Facebook and on LinkedIn, I'm Kristi Hines, not Kikolani. Only those who dug deep into my profiles were able to realize the connection.

The next conflict came when I started attending events, such as SMAZ, Arizona's best social media conference, and Blog World. When I would introduce myself to people, they would give me a blank stare for a moment. Then when I would say, "I'm Kikolani" and only then would they say: "Oh, ok, nice to meet you."

It happened again when I started branching out beyond blogging. I found myself wanting to target more than just one group of people. With my photography, I wanted to create a community of local photographers and expand into anyone interested in photography.

So what did I do? I began building photography community under the brand @kristihines on Twitter. And that was fine, for a while. Then I started to develop myself as a freelance writer, with the goal of becoming an online marketing consultant. This would ideally go under @kristihines with the expanded network that I have on @kikolani. I have two branded personas that I would love to combine into one, but I can't. It's too late.

Instead, I've had to figure out how to blend my freelancing with my blogging oriented audience, and redirect anyone who finds me @kristihines to @kikolani. So far, it seems to be working okay – I can cross-reference both profiles right in my Twitter bio. But this whole dilemma could have been avoided altogether if I had originally built my brand on @kristihines and then branched out into different interests from there.

Start Your List from Day One

The next thing I would change is to start a mailing list from day one. I don't see the mailing list as a way to make money through affiliate marketing or product creation, but rather a way to connect directly with my audience.

If you have followers on Twitter that are following tens of thousands of people, they might miss your message. But if you are sending your message right to their email box, you will stand a much better chance of being heard.

Most people are a little shy about creating a list from the beginning. The number one thought that held me back (and probably holds others back as well) is why, with only 10 subscribers to my RSS feed would I need a mailing list? If I only have 10 folks on a mailing list, what's the point?

The point is this: When I started out, I had a completely different set of followers than I do today. Some of my original followers are still with me, which is a pretty amazing, but some I lost contact with over the years. I truly feel that if I had a stronger connection them, through the direct contact of an email list, that more of those original followers would be with me today.

What is the key? Your mailing list can't be one that only sells, sells, and sells. If the only time you send out a newsletter is when you are promoting a new product of yours or someone else's, you are *not* engaging with your audience. You're mining them, and they will start categorizing your communications as junk, or maybe unsubscribe entirely.

To engage with your audience through your mailing list, you must give them a little something extra. You have to send them more content. Exclusive content. Even if it is something simple, like a great tip you haven't shared on your blog, or expanding upon idea that you shared publically to be more valuable for your subscribers.

I do a lot of freelance writing, and I often write about business topics, since business blogs are generally the ones that pay for writers. So one thing I can do easily on my email list (which is composed mostly of personal bloggers) is send my subscribers a little bonus by tailoring the strategies I have written for a business audience for my blogging audience. It is repurposing content at its finest, and the perfect way to engage with my mailing list.

The best part of this approach is you can do it too, from day one, with only 10 people on your list!

Don't Get Involved with the Wrong Crowd

I pride myself in the fact that I feel I have a pretty open mind about everything, and look for the best in everyone. One of the things that can happen to open minded people, especially ones that start out as simply bloggers looking to one day grow into a business, is getting mixed up with the wrong crowd.

The wrong crowd, especially when you're entering the online world for the first time, is hard to spot. It may just be one person or a group of people. When they take you under their wing, they seem perfect; always supportive of what you do, almost to the point of smothering you, like a parent proud of their child's achievements.

You'll only know that you're in the wrong crowd when their true colors begin to emerge. They start to tell you that you shouldn't bother with John Smith because he's too popular and doesn't care about you, or with Jane Doe because she's only interested in her own success. Of course, since they have been so wonderful to you, you figure that they only have your best interests in mind.

Then they start to write posts against John Doe and Jane Smith, ripping into their blogs, strategies, products, or services. What you'll begin to realize, at this point, is that all of the people they are blasting are people who are more successful than they are. You'll begin to realize that if they spent half the time working on their own strategies and image that they spend complaining about others, they would be more successful.

This is the point where you'll want to make a run for it. You'll start separating yourself from this crowd, and take a closer look at the Johns and Janes, who aren't so bad once you let go of what everyone else said about them. Of course, when you do this, you'll see that you need to focus more on your own growth and build a community that is supportive and positive.

Once you begin this shift, you will start to become more successful. Then you will really see that negative crowd for who they are. They might even start to inflict their negativity on you. At this point, you just have to let them go about their business. You can't stop them, and the time you spend trying to defend yourself will just be wasted time that you could be spending with positive mentors who really care about your success instead of calling you a sellout.

Remember that there is nothing wrong with you just because your goal in life is to be successful at doing something you love. Anyone who attacks people who strive to be better at what they do or be more successful than they are is not the right person to be associated with. You want to be around people who are happy for your success and the success of others. Anyone else will simply guide you in the wrong direction.

Kristi Hines (@kikolani, @kristihines) is a freelance writer, online marketing consultant, and blogger at Kikolani.
<u>*Started Audience Building*</u>*: 2009*
<u>*Blogs and Websites*</u>*: Kikolani.com; KristiHines.com; Photostry.com*
<u>*Our Favorite Blog Post*</u>*: Spy on your Competition*

Linda Bustos: Make Yourself Indispensable

Make yourself absolutely and completely indispensable through purpose, differentiation, and flexibility.

I first came on board with Get Elastic as a contractor, writing twice per week. At that time, the blog had a few hundred subscribers and was focused on the company: the product, research and development and other company news.

Elastic Path wanted a change, and brought me on to write more general articles on the e-commerce industry.

After few weeks I was offered a full-time position, to dedicate 100% of my efforts to the blog, writing 5 posts per week. This, along with social networking efforts (back in 2007, that meant StumbleUpon, Reddit, and networking with other e-commerce bloggers), helped the blog readership to grow to 500, then 1,000+ readers in only a few months. Today, we have over 13,000 daily readers.

Many business blogs are at a disadvantage here, because they don't have a full-time blogger who can make the blog their only focus – if you've got another job to do, it's almost impossible to maintain frequent, high-quality blog content. It simply isn't your priority, and you can't expect great results.

I tend to take an instructional, almost textbook tone when I'm writing – it fits the nature and goals of our blog, and established me as an authority on the subject matter. It doesn't provoke a lot of serious engagement, but that's just fine for Get Elastic. It's more important for us to have the social proof that comes with a large audience, and it provides a great resource for our sales people who can nurture leads by showing them our dedication to new thoughts and concepts in the ecommerce industry.

For me, meeting and getting to know other bloggers was an amazing thing – there were so many interesting, talented people out there with whom I could exchange information. There was some mutual back and forth linking going on, and we shared an interested readership. I believe referrals from these established bloggers helped us grow our readership, as people trust word-of-mouth recommendations.

So that's how I got to where I am – not your usual start-up story, I know!

But if you were to be starting from scratch, I would like to suggest a few things to help get you on your way...

Start With Preparation

Before launching your blog, you should have at least ten posts ready and waiting to go.

You don't really know how busy you're going to be once you launch, and if you want to do any effective networking, there should be good content on your site for people to look at. Otherwise the people you approach will feel that you are completely self-serving, and not really interested in them – and that just makes you look bad. If you need to launch first, allow yourself enough time to publish that many articles before you start networking!

I try to keep my editorial calendar filled weeks, if not months in advance. It makes my life easier, keeps me focused on what's going to be happening, let's me outline my goals – there are dozens of good reasons to prepare well in advance.

Have a Purpose

Before launching, make sure that you have a strong value proposition for your blog. You should know exactly why you're blogging and what you want and need to get out of it for it to be worth your time. Are you going to be teaching or offering opinion? Do you want to generate sales, or be a thought leader?

It's harder to gain subscribers to a blog now that Twitter and Facebook are around. It used to be that if you had, say, 4 hours to spend on the net, you'd spend most of them reading and commenting on blogs. Now, you'll probably spend three of those hours on Twitter looking a content that has been pre-screened by your connections.

There has to be a really, really good reason for someone to want to see your content regularly instead of waiting for it to be shared with them by a friend. Spend time on making that reason a good one!

Research and Differentiation

The internet is a pretty big place, but it's also a pretty crowded place. Unless you're in a very exclusive niche, you're going to want to think long and hard before starting your blog. In busy spaces, like marketing or design, you have to really make sure you've got something new to say – you have to make yourself an indispensable resource. Try to talk about things that nobody else is talking about in that industry.

So... growth?

No matter what your niche is, the process of growing an audience is pretty much the same for everyone. I know that in the e-commerce space, we're all doing basically the same thing:

- ✓ Posting great content,
- ✓ Sharing great content – ours and others,
- ✓ Linking to good resources,
- ✓ Sharing our opinions,
- ✓ Maintaining a consistent voice and approach,
- ✓ Engaging in thought leadership – changing the way we and our readers think about our industry.

The GetElastic blog is known for providing content without an agenda – we share our thoughts and ideas without serious expectations. We can do this because I'm a full time, dedicated blogger. Our readers know me, and have developed trust.

Trust – there's an important word. It is far more important to have the trust of your readers than to have their comments or even their business.

What About Engagement?

You see, whether or not you need your readers to be engaged, and in what way, depends on why you wanted them in the first place. Remember that preparation section above? You may need an audience in the hundreds of thousands, but it may not matter at all whether they comment on your posts as long as they tweet them or buy your products.

Personally, I think that comments are over-rated, and I'd take social sharing over comments any time. Word of mouth is the most effective way to get your message out there, and it's great for SEO. Also, few people actually read all of the comments, and those people who receive your posts via email or RSS often don't click through to your website and never see them at all.

If after all of this, you're still set on having a blog – good for you, it can be a constantly challenging and very rewarding project. If you create great content, and work diligently at networking and getting it read, then eventually, you will have an audience – so what are you going to do with it?

For me over at GetElastic, having a blog with thousands of subscribers works as excellent social proof. If that many people are interested in what we have to say, then it must be worth looking at. For the blog, our goal was thought leadership – our actual for-profit business comes after that.

When to Pull the Plug

But there are many other reasons you could want an audience – it might be your main source of customers, it could be validation of your work or thinking, it could be personally fulfilling for you to be creating and sharing content. There is really no bad reason to want an audience for your blog, as long as you show respect for your readers and the people you connect with.

Sometimes though, even good things must come to an end, and it's as important to know when to stop blogging as to know how to start.

When you start running out of ideas, when the return on the investment of your time decreases, when you get bored – these are all signs that it's time to bow out. When you're first planning and preparing for your blog, decide what it would take for you to quit. When that situation presents itself – follow through.

You have to be willing to change your tactics; to innovate and experiment. If something isn't working right – well, you know what they say about repeating the same thing expecting different results.

 *Linda Bustos (@GetElastic) is the full-time blogger for GetElastic.com, and director of e-commerce research for The Last Half software, an e-commerce software platform for digital goods and publishing companies.*
Start of Audience Building: 2007
Blogs and Websites: GetElastic.com; ElasticPath.com
Our Favorite Blog Post: Four Social Behaviors Invading Ecommerce

Natalie Sisson: The Power of One

Give and give and give and give.

It seems like so long ago that my blogging audience was comprised of one lovely reader following what I wrote. I remember being so excited and nervous about pushing `publish' on my first post. For some reason I expected it to be a big deal. And it was…to me. Me and my best friend; that was my entire audience.

Fast forward to present day, and I have a thriving community of fellow Suitcase Entrepreneurs, and those living, or wanting to live, a freedom based lifestyle. I still pinch myself, that since those humble days, I've been lucky enough to grow such an amazing tribe, and as a result I've been asked to blog for Forbes, Young Entrepreneur, Under30CEO, the Nike Women Make Yourself Movement and many more.

I quickly realized that a blog is nothing without an engaged audience that guides the blogger's journey to becoming a better writer, connector and provider of massive value. My tribe has shaped a lot of what I write about and offer. They have been my cheering squad on the days when I've felt like giving up. I thrive off their feedback and engagement, which drives most of what I do on the SuitcaseEntrepreneur.com.

Simply put, Rome was not built in a day. Neither is a thriving and engaged community of people who tune in to your blog weekly to read what you have to say, and to soak up your knowledge, your how-to articles, and believe in what you say because it resonates so deeply with them.

The Key Lessons Learned

Like many people, when you start your blog you should hit up all your friends via email and ask them to come and visit, or share it with their friends. Then you look to Facebook, and send a message to a few key people that have some 'Klout', telling them why you're passionate about getting your message out to a bigger crowd.

You post on your wall, you update your LinkedIn status and you tell everyone you meet about why they should come and visit your blog. And then you sit back and say `My work here is done'.

If you believed that then you'll believe anything.

The cold hard truth is that a community takes a lot of consistent effort to build; a lot of hard work, epic content and continual promotion. You are essentially your own brand and you have to learn the pillars of marketing to ensure you remain relevant and visible in a crowded online world.

I learned early on that if all I did was promote my blog online, I'd turn people away. I made those common mistakes of spamming my own wall with links to my blog posts 2-3 times per day and posting continual updates about my blog. I even had friends send me messages admiring my enthusiasm but telling me to get a life and post about other things from time to time.

I also tried writing content that was fun, friendly and popular including standard boring headlines that really sent the message of `Hey, I'm mediocre and if you visit my blog that's precisely what you'll find more of.'

Months later I learned that what drove the most traffic to my site – and caused them to stick around – was being myself, letting my humor and quirkiness shine through, ranting, being provocative, having a strong opinion and, most of all, owning it when I screwed up. There's nothing like vulnerability and letting people in to why you failed, and then giving your advice on how they can avoid doing the same, to get a crowd on your side.

You can actually hear them say "I get to see the real you, and that I can connect with, understand, and see a part of me in". That's when you've really hit the nail on the head and developed a tribe of adoring fans and advocates.

The Wise Owl Does It This Way

With an engaged audience comes great responsibility.

You must treat them like stars, roll out the red carpet, and continue to get to know more about what makes them tick. Remember that they are your lifeline. They make you what you are. The share your content and they put you up on the platform that allows you to spread your message to the world.

So what do I do differently now from when I started out? I have a purpose and a big vision, amplified by my goals and specific tactics that I apply to my blog and my business.

I now write at least 3 times a week about topics defined by the many months of research and feedback that I've asked for and received from my tribe. I have an editorial calendar so I know what's coming up, how relevant and timely it is and how it works in with major events, holidays, product and program launches, as well as my world travels.

I can see not only what's going up on my blog but what webinars I'm running, what content I'm putting in my newsletter, what online tool I'll introduce by video each Tuesday. I also know which podcast interview is due to be published and what promotions I'm doing or supporting someone else in.

I aim to write in chunks at a time, so I can line them up for the week ahead. I tend to write every single day regardless, as these days I'm asked to write a lot of guest posts. I'm always creating. I'm always recording what I do where possible, to document it and see if there's a way I can turn it into something valuable for my tribe.

I edit a lot more, I encourage comments on my blogs, I thank people who share my content personally, and I highlight new members of my community on Facebook and in my newsletter. I aim to put their personal business challenges into case studies on my blog. I seek to bring more of them into everything I do.

I also get away from it all by reading books outside my realm of professional interest, to expand my horizons and give me some perspective on what I do. More importantly, I find time to shake my booty to great music to have some fun and keep the creative juices flowing when I'm working! You should too.

My Step By Step Audience Building Checklist

If I had to do it all over again I'd be way more strategic, from the beginning.

Building an audience of like-minded people is all about nurturing relationships – by knowing what they need and providing them with the answers, solutions, insight and genuine examples.

Sure, I started off building my tribe in an ad-hoc, enthusiasm-driven way, but in an ideal world, but just because that's what I did doesn't mean that you have to!

Here is what I aim to do each day or week, and what I recommend as a step by step approach to building an engaged audience:

Google Reader

✓ Read the latest top blogs in business and social media

✓ Make sure to comment on 5 or more each day, and then share them via Twitter or Facebook

✓ Check RSS feed for LinkedIn Answers for Small Business, and endeavor to answer at least three

✓ Look at Google Alerts for Suitcase Entrepreneur and Natalie Sisson, and respond accordingly

Mail Chimp

✓ Check stats on my email campaigns and click through rates weekly, and optimize the content

✓ Write and send one weekly Highflyer newsletter (preferably with offer/incentive every third)

✓ Respond to personal emails sent in reply to my `Introduce yourself' email

Forum Interaction

✓ Visit the following forums to read their content, answer questions and connect with new people: Blogher, SethGodin, Linchpin, Under30CEO, Tropical MBA Mastermind, Think Traffic, Women Entrepreneurs, Savour the Success, Small Business Brief, Business.com Answers

ENGAGEMENT FROM SCRATCH!

Facebook

- ✓ Leave an intelligent comment on two pages per day
- ✓ Tag 1-3 new pages on my page each week
- ✓ Work on one new promotion strategy each month to add more fans

Twitter

- ✓ Follow 40-50 new entrepreneurs that are in line with my values each week, via Twellow
- ✓ Converse and engage with 10 people per day

YouTube

- ✓ Add 10 new people as friends in the business arena and comment on their channels
- ✓ Upload one new video a week and submit to TubeMogul
- ✓ Send each new video to 25 subscribers who'd be interested, and ask them to share

LinkedIn

- ✓ Connect with 5-10 more interesting women entrepreneurs, and direct them to my blog
- ✓ Submit new blog posts to appropriate groups
- ✓ Skim through groups and contribute to 5 interesting discussions

Relationship Marketing

- ✓ Introduce at least 2 people in my network that would benefit from knowing each other – either via email, Twitter, Facebook or LinkedIn
- ✓ Submit at least two guest posts per month to major sites that would increase my visibility
- ✓ Say yes to as many interview requests, radio shows or guest blog opportunities as possible

As you can probably tell, this is a whole heap of effort and time to invest! I view it as part of my blog and business building activities. It is part of my marketing, sales and customer service rolled into one.

Give, give and give in every way possible, and ye shall receive in droves.

Natalie Sisson (@NatalieSisson, @WomanzWorld) is a suitcase entrepreneur showing the world how to live the life they want, and run their businesses, too.
Started Audience Building: 2006
Websites and Blogs: NatalieSisson.com, SuitcaseEntrepreneur.com
Our Favorite Blog Post: Why the Money Really is in the Email List

Steve Kamb: One Email at a Time

Build your audience, one fan at a time.

Starting to build a new audience from scratch seems like a daunting task; after all, how do you lead without any followers?

The absolute first step that I would take would be to pick a topic that has 100% of my passion and attention. I've read plenty of blogs that were obviously written by somebody whose heart wasn't in it; when you can tell that a blog was created solely for the money, it's not a blog I would care to read, and not somebody I would want to learn from.

So, I'd start by writing about things that interest me, which ensures that I won't get bored or run out of topics quickly. Most importantly, I'm picking something that I will actually enjoy working on during the months upon months of work with zero payoff. I know I need something that I would enjoy doing whether I had two people reading it or two hundred thousand.

Insanely Useful, For Free

After having picked a topic on something that I felt incredibly passionate about, I would bust my butt to give away as much incredibly useful and helpful content, completely for free. I realize that because I will have just started completely from scratch, nobody will have any clue who I am or why they should listen to me; it's going to take months and months of consistently cranking out high-quality articles that are helpful to people.

With my current venture, I wrote for eighteen months and gave away something like 250 articles before asking for anything at all in return other than my audience's attention; I would expect to do the same this time around – give, give, give. I want to become the guy known for giving away insane amounts of free content.

Now, as I give away all of this free content, I'm going to start establishing relationships with bloggers that I truly admire – leaving well thought-out comments on their blogs, emailing them with no end goal other than letting them know that I'm a fan of their work, and asking for nothing else. Once a relationship has been established, I'd continue to send them the occasional email, forwarding them articles that might be helpful to their community and connecting with them on Twitter. The goal is to be as helpful as possible to them so my name becomes synonymous amongst my readers and peers as a guy that just wants to help.

Now, after I've given away a clinically insane amount of free content that is well written, passionate, and full of helpful information, some of it will start to make its way around the internet via word of mouth and social media. In order to turn those initial readers into passionate followers, I would work extra hard to personally connect with each and every one of them.

My Very First Comment

I will never forget the first person to ever leave a comment on my current website. His name is Evan, and he's from California: he does muay thai, directs short films, and lives with his family in San Francisco. I know this because I took the time to email Evan and thank him for reading. I also asked him how he found my site, what he was working on, what else he wanted me to write about, and how I could help him in any way possible.

I did this for probably the first six months of my site – I emailed every single person that left a comment…and not a canned "thanks for commenting!" email, but an email that showed that I actually cared. After all, they took the time to leave a comment and read my work, it was the least I could do.

It's these personal relationships that turn bloggers from a random writer on the Internet into somebody that your readers want to become emotionally invested in.

So, as long as I had the capacity to do so, I would continue to reach out personally to each and every commenter for as long as possible – these early adopters will become the people that help spread the word to their friends, and nothing is more important this day and age than a ringing endorsement from a friend.

After all, when was the last time you bought something without at least a quick "hey, I'm thinking of buying this or reading that, what do you think?"

Become an Authority

As I continue to email readers and focusing on writing great content, I'm going to keep building my relationships with other bloggers, doing everything I can to help them out. After a decent period of time, if any of the bloggers that I've been communicating with allow guest posts on their site, I would then start working on a killer blog topic and outline that is 100% perfect for their audiences.

After establishing myself as an authority and pulling in new readers, I want to make it incredibly easy for new readers to figure out who I am and what I stand for – I'll take a stance on a few important issues and let new folks know what we believe in as a community (not just me, but ALL of us). Sure, I'll probably alienate some folks who haven't different viewpoints, which is exactly what I'm hoping for - weeding out the "maybes" and attracting the people that say "hell yeah!" This is the passionate foundation that will build the future of the community.

As the size of the site grows, I would start to adjust my writing, opting for "us," "we," and "our" instead of "me," "I" and "mine." I want to be one of the guys in the community, just piece of a machine that is all working in unison towards the goal of the site (a better life, improved whatever, a passion for this/that, etc.) When you give people an opportunity to be part of something, to include them in the group and show that you truly value their input and opinion, they're going to be proud of what they've helped create; sharing this with their friends is no longer "hey look at this cool site" but rather "hey I'm part of this cool group, you should come see what we're all about!"

If this sounds too complicated...

But let's say that all of this sounds like way too much work, or way too much reading. I'll break things down into even simpler terms:

Want to know how to build a passionate fanbase from scratch? The answer is one fan at a time.

One email at a time.

Cherish each and every reader, and let them know that you appreciate them taking the time out of their day to check out your site. Give your passion and attention to your readers; be careful though, it's very contagious and can spread like wildfire at a moment's notice.

Steve Kamb (@SteveKamb) is the creator of Nerd Fitness, dedicated to helping "desk jockeys, nerds and average Joes level up their lives!"
<u>Start of Audience Building</u>: *2008*
<u>Blogs and Websites</u>: *NerdFitness.com*
<u>Our Favorite Blog Post</u>: *What the Hell are You Waiting For?*

Are you enjoying the book?
Are you finding it valuable?

If you are, then why not share the love?

The book is cheap (on Amazon.com), or free (if you download it digitally on the book's website at EngagementFromScratch.com) – so why not give it as a gift to someone you care about?

Or if you don't want to do that (and haven't already), could you take a few minutes to write a review on Amazon.com?

There's no marketing department behind this book, and no powerful bookseller driving it to the top off the charts – if it's going to succeed, it will be because of readers just like you.

And hey, it's not like there's a big payout for me if you do – the digital copy is free, and 50% of the profits from book sales go to the Network for Teaching Entrepreneurship.

So… can you take a few minutes to help out?

Please?

Pretty please?

I knew I could count on you!

Thanks in advance. Your help means a lot to me, and I really appreciate it!

www.EngagementFromScratch.com

Section 7: Step-By-Step

Finally, it's time to bring it all together into checklists and step-by-step processes that you can follow, to put everything you've learned up until now into practice.

Ana Hoffman's contribution, "Not All Blogs Are Created Equal", explains that above all else, you must be a doer, not a spectator.

Dino Dogan's post, "How to Create a Community of Fanatics", tells you that you must be a human, deliver the goods, and have some fun.

Jeff Bullas's essay, "Building a Global Engaged Audience", teaches you that careful planning and quality execution leads to success.

Jk Allen's article, "Six Tips to Build an Engaged Audience from Scratch", reminds you that every teacher was once a student.

Steve Scott's contribution, "12 Steps to Building an Engaged Audience", explains that above all else, working hard is not optional.

Tyler Tervooren's essay, "The Fundamentals are Timeless", teaches you to be a leader, show humility, be consistent, and move forward.

Without further ado, let's get to it... the step-by-step processes that these audience builders recommend for growing an engaged audience, from scratch.

Ana Hoffman: Not All Blogs Are Created Equal

Be a doer, not a spectator.

Not all blogs are created equal.

Some blogs take off like wild fire within weeks of their creation, and some might take months (or longer) to even start seeing the light of day.

Your blog might be one of the latter ones. You write great content, yet your competitor's blog with mediocre posts seems to get all the traffic.

That's because not all blogs are created equal.

When Guy Kawasaki created his blog, he had the benefit of already being a famous persona in business and online. No wonder he had nearly 4,000 daily visitors within weeks.

Chances are you are not Guy Kawasaki.

But that's okay, because neither was I.

So now, you and I can have a real heart to heart on ***how to REALLY create a popular blog, starting with nothing***.

In the beginning, there was... hard work!

No other way around it. No silver bullet. No secrets.

Just plain old-fashioned *"let's drink lots of good coffee and stay up at all hours of the night, work around your family schedule and any other commitments you might have"* kind of work.

And start from the beginning.

The Best Bloggers Are Natural Hackers

Traffic Generation Cafe isn't the first or the only blog to talk about website traffic generation. There are plenty others that paved the way.

Yet, here I am, alive and kicking – and growing!

164

What's my secret?

You know that phrase "*think outside the box*"? I hate it. There's no such thing as the dreaded "box". *You* are the only box that you need to worry about.

You see, all great bloggers are natural hackers. They took a good look around, measured themselves up against their competition, and went against the grain.

Do you have what it takes?

The very first question you have to ask yourself is this:

"Is my blog worth reading?"

Is your content AWESOME and unique? Is it infused with personality? Does it help your reader to solve THEIR problems?

The opposite of the above would be:

- ✓ Your content is generic and can be found on every other blog in your niche.
- ✓ You don't offer any unique point of view on your blog.
- ✓ You don't have a "hook" that would keep your readers coming back (usually, the best hook is a mixture of personality and a unique angle at solving your readers' problems).
- ✓ You focus on the things that *you* are interested in, and don't provide any solutions to your visitors.

Start there.

Examine your blog as impartially as you can. Ask a friend. Ask me. Ask someone to take a look at your content and give you an *honest* opinion.

Don't do anything until you get over this hurdle.

Find Your Voice

The best voice you can give to your blog is the one that you *already* have.

Don't create a blogging "persona" that is a far cry from who you really are. If you do that, you'll only be able to keep it going for so long, and it will eventually become a weight that drags you down.

Example: I am not a story-teller. I don't do fancy. I am generally not good with words. Especially considering that English is not my first language.

What I am good with is giving *straight actionable advice*. I speak my mind, and I do it well.

I didn't realize that until my first blog became an obvious flop. I got tired pretty quickly of trying to be the kind of writer I really wasn't, and my readers noticed. Soon enough I started hearing crickets, and that's when I knew it was time to reinvent myself... to simply go back to what I knew how to do best.

Now let's get down to business: *the "Hows" of building an engaged audience from scratch*.

1. Create Pillar Content Right Off the Bat

Your first step is to write, write, write.

Don't do anything else – just write.

Edit yourself without mercy.

Come up with brilliant ways to write about the same old stuff that everybody else is writing (if you can't come up with anything fresh) from an entirely different point of view.

Provoke your readers' minds.

My very first post on TGC was a humongous list of 202 Bite-Sized Tips To Insanely Increase Your Blog Traffic.

Why 202? No reason.

I just wanted to create the biggest list of its kind and I did. Needless to say, that brought me a lot of traffic right off the bat, and the post was mentioned on several prestigious blogs after that.

2. Create Social Proof

Have you ever visited a blog that was so quiet you weren't sure it was even alive? No comments, no tweets; just sitting there, lonely and forgotten...

Yes, I know, I am sad for the blogger as well.

Existing engagement encourages more engagement. And that, my friend, is what social scientists call *Social Proof.*

I do understand your dilemma though.

You have a new or fairly new blog that hasn't quite developed a following yet.

So how are you to prove to your visitors that you are worthy of their attention? How do you get that initial push, that first comment, first tweet?

That's where I come to the rescue. On a white horse and all.

- ✓ *Have enough posts:* Forget about bringing traffic to a blog with a couple of posts. Completely counter-productive.

- ✓ *Launch without comments:* If you blog is not getting much traffic or comments, post without comments first. As your traffic grows, you can always open the posts for discussion later.

- ✓ *Create a commenting tribe:* That's right: take the matter of no comments into your own hands. Create a group of like-minded peer blogs and start commenting on each other's posts.

- ✓ *Create more tweets:* Here's an easy way to create Twitter social proof: **have more than 1 Twitter account**! Or more than 2, or even more than 3. When I first started, I had (well, still technically do) *6 Twitter accounts*. To learn more about my Twitter strategy, read my post about How to Get Traffic from Twitter (Google it).

- ✓ *Create more Facebook shares:* It's even easier to get more Facebook shares. All you do here is find some existing niche tribes on Facebook (just search for "your keyword" plus the word "tribe"), join the fan pages, and start posting your links. Of course, it's good etiquette to not just spam the pages, but check out other posts as well.

- ✓ *Limit Choice of Social Sharing Buttons*: Don't ever display buttons that your readers aren't using. For instance, I noticed on my blog that I rarely get any Diggs. Since I am not an active Digg member and will never become anything close to a power player on that site, I simply removed that button from my blog.

3. Create Profitable Alliances

Call it what you want: alliance, partnership, JV – all roads lead to Rome.

This works no matter what stage your blog is in, how much perceived authority you, as a blogger, have, how big your readership is – the only thing that matters is *value*.

We all have something we do better than the next blogger, know more about something than the next guy – we all have something to offer that someone else might want or need.

So, working together with other bloggers to achieve the greater good…

Here's how to create those alliances:

1. Links / Mentions

One of the easiest forms of collaboration happens to be one of the most effective ones as well.

I've benefited greatly from it through creating more traffic from the mentioned blogs, as well as more comments – at the very least from the bloggers themselves, from being mentioned on their blogs in return, from referral business even, like consulting clients, blog audits, etc.

2. Promoting in a Post

Every once in a while, I like to highlight specific bloggers and the interesting projects they are currently working on.

3. Guest Posting

Yes, I can hold this note for a long time.

Imagine you'd like to network with a blogger who seems to be simply unapproachable because of his/her strong reputation in the blogging community. The kind of blogger you really would love to get to know better, in other words.

You can't and shouldn't just send them an email, however nice it might be, introducing yourself and letting them know you are after a piece of their attention.

Of course, not.

But submit an awesome blog post, start commenting on their blog, and sooner than later they know who you are and you are on an email basis with them. That's a sweet spot to be in!

4. Making Introductions

That happens all the time.

You know someone I want to know? Requesting an introduction is in order – assuming, of course, that I already networked with you, linked to you, and am on a first name basis with you.

5. Swap Ads

Simple enough, but with a twist.

Find a blog with an untapped audience!

Don't just go to a blogger you are already sharing the readership with. Find someone whose content doesn't compete, but rather compliments yours.

Then approach them with the idea to swap ads and "exchange" traffic.

5. Offer your freebie as a bonus!

Know someone with a great product, and think your freebie will make a great bonus to it?

Everyone loves a good bonus and as long as it's not in competition with the product, this should be an easy deal to make.

6. Co-Registration

Get some bloggers with great newsletters together and start promoting each other on a Thank You page that your new subscribers will see right after they sign up to your list.

"…I think you'd really love to check out these newsletters I subscribe to and know to provide tremendous value:…"

7. Product Co-Creation

Yes, everyone wanting to make any serious money online needs their own product at some point.

Having a hard time with that idea? Have no clue how to even approach it?

Partner with someone who is in the same boat – two heads are better than one.

Better yet, find someone who already has an idea or is in some stages of development of a product, but needs your expertise to make it complete.

8. Special Discounts

Have a product already?

Offer a special discount to the readers of a particular blog.

Exclusivity is still a hot commodity, and will guarantee to bring you red-hot traffic ready to buy.

9. Run a Contest

This one is definitely better done with a partner or two – less work, better results.

The really hard part is attracting some strong sponsors; connections are the key here. However, if you've done the initial steps listed above and already positioned yourself as an authority figure in your niche, that shouldn't be a problem.

Let Your Readers Know Who You Are

Time and time again, I see this happen: a *faceless blog*.

No "Here's what you can learn on this blog...", no "Hi, I am so and so…", no "here what I am all about", no "feel free to get in touch with me".

Big mistake!

When I visit your blog, I – your average reader – want to see the man/woman behind the lines. I want to know if you are worth my attention. I want to know that, if I were to ask you a question, I would get an answer.

Your blog audience engagement starts with this:

1. Your "About Me" Page

This is a good place to talk about… well, you. Let your readers know who is behind your blog. Why are you blogging? What are you blogging about? Why should I read your blog?

Very important: *don't* get carried away.

Yes, it is a page about you, but not really. **It's still about your reader**. It's about you showing them that you are worth a look, a read, a comment.

It's still *all about them*.

2. Your "Contact Me" Page

Equally important: accessibility counts.

Here you add whatever you feel comfortable adding. Some ideas:

✓ Your phone number

✓ Your Skype, AOL, and Yahoo! messenger IDs

✓ Links to your social networking profiles (Twitter, Facebook, Google+, and the like)

✓ A "Contact Me" form (I use a plug-in called "Contact Form 73" on my blog, and there are plenty of others to choose from)

Your Next Step Is Your Call

You know why all blogs are not created equal?

Because some of them are created by doers and others are created by spectators.

Doers are people who read about it and then go do it. They are the go-getters, the bottom-liners, the achievers.

Spectators are people who read about it, but don't implement it. They are the side-liners, the "I could never do what she did" crowd, the eternal students.

The good news here is that you get to choose which camp you're in!

Traffic, traffic, traffic… Can't do without it, but don't know how to get it? Ana Hoffman (@SEOTrafficCafe) does, and she freely shares her best traffic generation advice that doesn't suck on her Traffic Generation Cafe blog. And don't forget to pick up Ana's 7 Steps to Complete Search Engine Domination free SEO report while you are at it – stop hoping for more search engine traffic and go get it!
<u>Start of Audience Building</u>: 2007
<u>Blogs and Websites</u>: Traffic Generation Cafe
<u>Our Favorite Blog Post</u>: 202 Bite-Sized Tips to Insanely Increase Your Blog Traffic

Dino Dogan: How to Create a Community of Fanatics

Be a human, deliver the goods, and have some fun.

I'm giving a keynote on the topic of creating a community of fanatics, so I've been spending a lot of time these past few weeks thinking about my contribution to this book, and the topic of creating an engaged audience.

This topic feels very alive and in-the-moment to me, simply because I'm in the midst of trying to manage a community of fanatics and I feel very much like a driver of a car with one missing wheel, speeding down the highway at 100 miles per hour.

But it didn't start that way. The community of fanatics wasn't supposed to be a community at all. But it turned into one... how?

Looking back, there are few fundamental principles that anyone could apply to their product, cause, brand, personality, etc. – If the right conditions are met, you just might end up with a community of fanatics. But why would you want to?

Why create a community of fanatics in the first place?

Those fanatically engaged members of your community are the ones that will market for you while you sleep. They will field technical questions from other members. They will fulfill your help-desk tickets. They will recruit other's to do the same. And they will do all this for free.

It's easy to stop there, and see the benefit of getting others to do your work for free, but let's follow this concept to its logical conclusion.

If someone is evangelizing on your behalf for free, that means they aren't doing it for money. And if they aren't doing it for money, they WHY are they doing it?

The answer is, they are doing it because they are passionate about you, your product, brand, cause, etc.

And when someone talks about you passionately and with enthusiasm, that enthusiasm acts as a cotagent and it infects everyone within an earshot.

This kind of enthusiasm CAN NOT be bought with money. But if you follow the fundamental principles laid out before you, you just might get it for free.

Principle #1: It Starts with Intention

It starts with your intention, but not the intention to create a community.

You can't spark a community by wanting to spark a community, any more than you could start a fire by wanting to start a fire.

When Dan Cristo and I started Triberr – which turned into an amazing community of bloggers and is the reason I was invited to contribute to this book – it wasn't because we wanted to start a community. Community simply emerged.

What we did do, is we set out to solve the biggest problem 99% of bloggers have. How do I get more eyeballs on my content?

That was the intention behind Triberr. No more, no less.

Currently recommended methods are bullshit. SEO takes so long that by the time you might see results, most bloggers have given up. Guest posting is a thankless, slave-like endeavor with no immediate payoff, and requires prolonged and concentrated effort to yield minimal results.

Triberr works immediately, and almost effortlessly. Not only that, but it is the engine which allows you to cement your core inner group of allies, whilst building an audience of your own.

New bloggers who have had no traffic will jump to thousands of hits per post immediately after joining Triberr.

Since Triberr has opened its doors in March of 2011, up until now (6 months later) we have sent hundreds of thousands of posts written by thousands of bloggers, via over 1 million tweets that were seen by billions of eyeballs.

So, the first lesson in building a community of fanatics is to create a new, effective, unique and original solution that solves a real pain-point for your target demographic. Which brings me to the second principle, and that is…

Principle #2: Know Your Audience

I'm a blogger solving my own problem.

There is an old marketing exercise where the goal is to create a customer avatar. This avatar is assigned gender, age, race, socio-economic status, locale, even name.

The point of this is to get into the mind of the customer, in order to understand his/her pain points, desires, passions, fears, etc.

When I conceived of Triberr, I also conceived of the ideal Triberr customer.

(Just in case you didn't know, Triberr is a free service, which makes certain higher functions available that can be engaged in using virtual currency called Bones. Bones are awarded to members, they can be won, or they can be purchased. So "customer" is the wrong word to use when describing Triberr community, but we'll use it as a catch-all for anyone who consumes what you're offering. Moving on…)

The avatar I created for Triberr is named Dino Dogan. He is a blogger. He is a good blogger who has had a hard time getting his content disseminated far and wide.

I understand Dino's fears. His frustrations. His pain-points. His passion. His desires. And we've made Triberr to solve Dino's problems.

Turns out, there are a lot of Dinos out there.

When we implement features for Triberr, we are simply solving our own problems. Both Dan and I are bloggers, and we understand the blogger's mind.

Which leads me to the next point, and that is…

Principle #3: Be a Human

No one wants to interact with a brand, a logo, a picture of your dog, or worse.

Communities are people. And people want to interact with other people.

So, let's cover some basics.

Use your own picture – and I mean a face, not a distant shot of you skydiving.

Use your real name. This one has much deeper implications, but using your real, full name simply means you're standing behind your words and actions.

Check your intentions. Whenever communicating with anyone at any time, this is a good thing to do. Why are you saying what you're saying? To sound cool? To cover up your mistake? To tell someone how much they suck and how right you are?

These are all bad intentions.

But if you're intention is to be helpful with no expectation of outcome, then those are some good intentions, my friend.

A community will expect a certain level of service from a real human. Be that human.

Which brings me to the Customer Service part of the equation.

Principle #4: Customer Service

First, I have to thank the airline industry, telephone industry, and banking industry, for taking the customer service expectations down to a virtual zero.

Because of them, you get points just for showing up and being human (see point number 3).

I discovered a funny thing about customer service while working on Triberr. People don't want to be lectured at. They don't want to be told what they could/should have done. They don't want to be treated like a task on your list.

What they do want is this: They want to be acknowledged immediately. You don't have to solve their issue right away, but they do want to know you've received their email and are working on it.

They want to be treated like a human being, and not like a number.

And they want their issue fixed. That's the bottom line. And the only thing that will fix their issue is if the issue goes away and everything goes back to being right.

This means you'll be doing a lot of work. Which brings me to point number 5.

Principle #5: Have Fun

There is a lot of hidden meaning in the phrase "have fun".

First, it means that community building will be a lot of work. And work is – by definition – NOT fun.

The only thing that makes work fun is if it gives us some meaning beyond the daily grind. And meaning is a hard thing to come by, especially if you're doing work for someone else.

If you're working for someone else, you are carrying out someone else's mission. For this, you will receive compensation. You get compensated because you are giving up a mission of your own.

As it stands, you may not even realize that there is a mission crouching somewhere deep inside you, just waiting to burst out.

You should find this mission and let it out. Only then will work have meaning, and it just might become fun as well.

Also, this applies to the community members. Your community should have fun participating in that community. Why should it be a grind?

To accomplish this, Triberr uses many principles taken from game mechanics and psychology. For example, every member has a Tribal Stream which shows posts published by everyone in your tribal network. You can vote (thumbs up/down) on posts in this stream and if you do, you just might win a Bone.

What kind of game mechanics is this?

Well, first, since the Tribal Stream is ephemeral (posts come and go) this gives an incentive for users to come back and check their stream several times a day. This is one of the reasons why Triberr.com has catapulted itself to number 1,032 most visited US websites in few short months and climbing (based on Alexa info).

The voting system uses the same gambling mechanics as a slot machine. You don't win a Bone every time you vote. That would become boring and monotonous and not fun very quickly.

Instead, you may win a Bone or two for every 5-15 votes you give. It's randomized using a fancy algorithm, and the voting became a game in and of itself as soon as we deployed it.

Being a member of the community should be fun for all, otherwise it's work, and work sucks.

Principle #6: Positioning

Positioning is shorthand. It's an easy and quick way for me to figure out what you are or are not.

Think 7-Up's marketing campaign when they used the slogan "7-Up. The Un-Cola".

You immediately know what 7-Up isn't, which helps you figure out what 7-Up is.

David and Goliath is a very popular and powerful positioning strategy. Even now as you're reading this, you're probably picturing David (the small guy) fighting Goliath (the big guy) in your mind.

Or Erin Brockovich (small guy) winning a lawsuit against a giant Gas company.

In fact, even though I wrote "David AND Goliath", you probably didn't picture David walking hand-in-hand with his best friend, Goliath.

Instead, you pictured a conflict between David and Goliath. That's how powerful that small-guy vs. big-guy positioning is.

Speaking of the Bible (David and Goliath is a story from the Old Testament), the entire God vs. Devil, good vs. evil story, is a story of Positioning.

1% of superstar bloggers receive 99% of the attention.

And attention = traffic.

Attention = book deals.

Attention = speaking engagements.

Attention = business opportunities.

Attention = money.

Superstar bloggers however, are not producing superstar content. Their content is safe, it's boring, it's rehashed, it's stale and regurgitated.

Meanwhile, there are amazing small bloggers producing incredible content and no one is reading it. Triberr's mission is to bring eyeballs to that content.

I don't think superstar bloggers and Goliath websites deserve the amount of attention they get. Small bloggers are infinitely more creative and interesting.

ENGAGEMENT FROM SCRATCH!

That is the Positioning story of Triberr.

What the Internet has done to democratize information, Triberr is doing to democratize attention.

 *Dino Dogan (@dinodogan) is co-founder of Triberr, and blogs at DIYBlogger.com.*
Started Audience Building: 2010
Websites and Blogs: Triberr.com; DIYBlogger.com
Our Favorite Blog Post: Chris Brogan's Blog Topics Suck! You're Welcome, Chris.

Jeff Bullas: Building a Global Engaged Audience

Careful planning and quality execution leads to success.

200 years ago, when you built a business, it was all about being local.

Today with the net, real-time communications, and easy to use social networks that have global reach, building a worldwide audience from scratch is within your grasp, and possible on a budget that was not feasible even 5 years ago.

There are some questions that will need to be answered in order to reach your goals:

- ✓ Where do you start?
- ✓ What tactics do you use?
- ✓ What tools are available that really work?

I'll cover six steps to building a global audience for your blog or business. We will look at:

1. Identifying your Passion and Innate Abilities
2. Creating a Plan and Strategy
3. Building the Blog and Blogging Basics
4. Creating Content that Engages
5. Marketing your Blog with Social Media
6. Maintaining Momentum

So let's get started!

Step One: Identify your Passion and Innate Abilities

Blogging is about writing, writing is hard work, and not everyone is cut out to put pen to paper or hunt keys on the keyboard for hours each day. Even Tolstoy, who may have been one of the greatest novelists of all time, once said: *"I don't like writing but I love having written"*.

ENGAGEMENT FROM SCRATCH!

It's like January 1st, when we clean the desk, set our goals and roll out the revised set of New Year's resolutions. Some of us are excited by the year ahead, and others are filled with dread, and are even wondering whether going back to "that" job is an option at all.

Motivation is a strange thing. For most of the industrial revolution and beyond we have used "external" motivations to drive ourselves and our employees to work and succeed. But there is a mismatch between what science knows and what business does.

We need to look at an approach built upon intrinsic motivation – a new "operating system" for the 21st century, that taps into our desire to do things:

- ✓ Because they matter;
- ✓ They are interesting; and
- ✓ Because they are part of something important.

In a study sponsored by the Federal Reserve Bank of America, scientists from the University of Chicago, MIT and Carnegie Mellon discovered that: *"In 8 out of 9 tasks examined across 3 experiments, higher incentives led to worse performance."*

In another study by the London School of Economics (the training ground of George Soros and the Alma Mater of 11 Nobel Laureates) scientists found, after watching 51 companies pay for performance plans, that: *"Most financial incentives can result in a negative impact on overall performance"*.

What science is telling us is that powerful, long-lasting motivation is built upon 3 elements.

1. Autonomy – the urge to direct our own lives.
2. Mastery – the desire to get better and better at something that matters.
3. Purpose – the yearning to do what we do in the service of something larger than ourselves.

10 years ago, no one would have thought that a professionally managed, heavily sponsored project (Encarta by Microsoft) to create a new media encyclopaedia would be comprehensively beaten to the ropes in a knockout by a free global social science experiment called "Wikipedia" involving thousands of unpaid volunteers working in their pyjamas from home.

What Should You Blog About?

People often ask me: "how do I know what I should blog about?" The answer seems simple; the secret lies in discovering what you love doing in combination with your innate talents. Easy to say, but sometimes very hard to discover.

A lot of people struggle their entire lives to discover what they should be doing as a career. Some people never discover the secret of making life a joyous journey, and for many, life is full of tedium doing things they hate.

It is a sad truth but many people go to their grave with their song unsung, and their talents and passions undiscovered.

Find Work That is Play

I recently came across a quote by the famous economist Dr. Paul Samuelson that encapsulates one of the secrets to success in life, business and blogging: *"Never underestimate the vital importance of finding early in life the work that for you is play. This turns possible underachievers into happy warriors."*

Most of us do not have the privilege of discovering this early on in life but stumble upon it years later. There is no rhyme or reason as to when or how this event occurs; it could be an epiphany or it could be a slow awakening, but if you discover it grab it with both hands. Do not ignore it – embrace it with all the energy and optimistic obsession that you can muster.

Work that is play is the combination of innate ability and aptitude combined with passion to create; a synergy that lubricates life's journey.

In his book "The Element," Sir Ken Robinson says this about discovering being in your Element: *"It is the place where the things we love and the things we're good at come together."*

Questions You Should Ask Yourself

So how do you find this element? What questions should you be asking to discover work that is play? Here are some questions you can start with:
- ✓ What comes easily to you?
- ✓ What do you read about till 2.30 in the morning?
- ✓ What gets you up at 4.30am?

- ✓ What do you enjoy doing?
- ✓ What kind of things do people compliment you on?
- ✓ What activities give your spirit energy?

You may find that that the topic of the blog that you create or the career that you love will be a combination of the answers to a few of these questions.

Step Two: Create a Plan and Marketing Strategy

A plan that will keep you on track, and ensure that you don't deviate towards dead ends or get distracted, is essential. If you really want to get serious, you could write a business plan and back that up with a marketing plan.

To keep it simple we will combine this into one overarching strategy; a strategy will ensure that you select the right tactics and tools to reach the right audience in the most efficient manner. In its simplest form, it involves 5 stages:

1. Identify Target Audience(s)

It is important to make sure that when you build your social networks, you have an audience that wants to *listen and engage*. Just because there are 2 billion people on the web doesn't mean they all want to listen to your message and story. For example, if you are selling wine then you will need to target restaurants, food bloggers and anyone who will help you reach an extended audience.

2. Set Goals

Goals keep you on track like a guided missile, but they need to be quantitative (how many) and timely. For example:

- ✓ Blog/website traffic goals
- ✓ 1,000 email subscribers in 6 month
- ✓ 2,000 Twitter followers in 3 months
- ✓ Sell 1,000 eBooks in the first 12 months at $19.95

3. Select Marketing Tactics and Tools to Achieve Goals

If your audience is on Facebook, for example, the marketing tactics you use could include:

- ✓ Installing a Facebook social plugin on the blog.

✓ Making it easy to 'like" your Facebook page from your daily/ weekly email newsletter or on your blog posts.

Brainstorm similar tactics for all of the other social media services you intend to use.

4. Monitor and Measure

It is important to monitor your success and your failures to see if people are subscribing or unsubscribing. This allows you to change tactics that aren't working, and find ones that do. Keep experimenting! Have quantifiable goals from the beginning will help you monitor and measure your progress as you follow your plans.

5. Rinse and Repeat

Now that you are finding what works and what doesn't you can focus on doing more of what does, and less of what doesn't. Of course, continue to keep an eye on your key performance indicators like sales per month, traffic and subscribers.

Step Three: Building the Blog and Blogging Basics

When I first started blogging, I made what were, in hindsight, some good decisions, and some bad decisions.

Good: I started my blog under my own name, JeffBullas.com, which was done, in part, to build a personal brand online.

Bad: I used the hosted version of WordPress at WordPress.com (not the WordPress that you get at WordPress.org and install on your own server) as my blogging platform, using their free hosted WordPress template. This ended up causing me more a lot more work later when I wanted to add extra features and functions. These are the decisions that can cost you a few pennies initially, but will save you a lot of time and grief later on.

So what are 12 blog building essentials?

1. Buy your Own Domain Name!

This is important because you can always take it with you and host your blog wherever you like. Sure, you use Blogger.com, TypePad.com and even

WordPress.com are all free, but it comes at the cost of your independence, and steals your flexibility to control your blogging destiny. They give you a domain name that is a subset of their domain and you can't move to a new domain without starting all over again. Your readers will have trouble finding you because you have moved.

So if you're serious about being a blogger, buy a domain – don't rent one! If you intend to create a strong personal brand to provide a platform for you as an thought leader, expert, author, musician, or consultant, a domain name that strongly reflects your personal name will help you get found online. If you are using the blog as marketing platform for a product, then of course it should be named and branded consistently with the product. And corporate blogs should be consistent with the company brand's look and feel, and should be a part of the company website.

2. Purchase a WordPress Template

WordPress dominates the world of blogging and you can buy templates ready to go for $40-$50. I use the WordPress template 'Frugal' (which has now been replaced by the upgraded version called Catalyst) – it is easy to use, especially as a non technical user. It requires no programming and makes it easy for me to do what I do best: blog.

There are myriad free and low cost templates for the WordPress content management system. Do your research and find one that will work your you, your company and your audience.

3. Hire a Good Web Designer

A good web designer will ensure that you have a web design that *works*, so that you can present the most professional brand you can afford to the online world. It is the global front door for your digital online brand.

In 1996, Steve Jobs, in an interview with Wired Magazine, said this about design: "*Design is a funny word. Some people think design means how it looks. But of course if you dig deeper, it's really how it works. The design of the Mac wasn't what it looked like, although that was part of it. To design something really well, you have to get it. You have to really grok what it's all about. It takes a passionate commitment to really thoroughly understand something, chew it up, not just quickly swallow it. Most people don't take the time to do that.*"

According to the Oxford English Dictionary, to "grok" something means *"to understand intuitively or by empathy; to establish rapport with"* and *"to empathize or communicate sympathetically with*).

So don't get lost in how it *looks*. Make sure it *works*.

The thing to remember here is that a blog is about content. If you have a video blog, making sure the videos are easy to view and play is paramount. If you have a text blog, making your posts clear and easy to digest is.

I have seen many blogs where the writing is so small that I can barely read the text, or the background provides little or no contrast, and you have to squint.

Don't give the reader an excuse to click away from your blog.

4. Choose Your Medium

Some people are much better speaking on video, some are better with written words. Find the medium that suits you best. Use the medium that lets your passion shine. Also you may find that you are good at both so you can mix it up and provide a variety of media. Video blogs are certainly becoming popular as some members of Gen Y and Generation I (Internet) would rather chew off their left arms than read a paragraph of text.

5. Provide Social Media Share Buttons

I remember a comment on my blog where a reader had suggested that I include a share button for LinkedIn, as he wanted to send my post to several hundred of his LinkedIn connections but had found it too difficult. A share button provides a low friction (2 clicks and you are 'shared' to hundreds of people) means for people to share without cutting and pasting headlines, links and opening software.

Include Twitter and Facebook share buttons, as a minimum. For extra credit, there's Google+ and LinkedIn.

6. Allow Readers to Subscribe via RSS and Email

Allowing people to subscribe to your blog by email and RSS is important; it will "push" new content to your readers' email inboxes or Google Readers every time you post. This promotes loyal readership, drives daily traffic, and makes sure that you are not forgotten. And it caters to audience preferences – some people *prefer* to read posts in their email inbox.

7. Provide Buttons For People to Subscribe To Your Social Media Channels

The minimum recommendation here is Facebook and Twitter, which will allow people to become not just consumers of your content, but part of your social network. Google+ is probably a good idea as well.

8. Regularly Publish Content to your Blog

Write, film or record your posts regularly, preferably once a day 5 days a week.

You will find that the top bloggers have this routine and discipline. If you can't commit to that, schedule at least one update per week, and be consistent. Remember that blogging is a form of publishing, and if readers show up and find nothing but old posts, they will not come back. Magazines and newspapers publish consistently and on time. Considering all of the difficulty they have, there is no excuse for a lack of timely new content on your blog!

9. Display Credibility Banners

This is a bit of a chicken and egg scenario. How do you, as a new blogger, showcase your expertise when you're just starting out? You'll want to use all of the offline credibility that you have at your disposal.

If you have any awards, degrees, certifications or publications that can be highlighted on the front page of your blog then get banners made. If you have written an article in a magazine, a book, been on a TV show, or won awards, then make sure that the web world can see it when they visit. When your Twitter followers and subscribers start to reach a few hundred, start displaying those numbers as well.

These "attention quantification" numbers are becoming more and more influential to readers and viewers, so forget about modesty – tell people how many other people are into what you're saying.

10. 'About' or 'Bio' Menu Tab

Blogs still are personal, unless you're the Huffington Post or Mashable. Readers want to know who you are and what you have done. They want to identify with you and start to connect. So your About will open to a page on your blog where you will provide your biography in summary. Also include any interesting facts about yourself that a potential reader could make a connection with, such as "off-topic" hobbies or interests.

11. Good Headlines

You only have a few seconds before the reader decide whether they want to read your post or not, so a headline that compels and teases blog and tweet readers to get to the end of your post. List posts such as "10 Best Ways To..." or "The 5 Top ..." or "How To..." are always effective. These might seem overused, but the fact remains they work. We will look at this in more detail later on.

12. Social Comment System That Displays Comments and Reactions

The comment component for a blog is a major feature of blogging that many content management systems offer as a standard feature. There are other systems such as Disqus that you can install to increase comment functionality and add things like ranking, and social media reactions. Since beginning to use Disqus, I have found that my comment counts have increased. It also allows people to post comments with their social channel IDs rather than just an email address, which is good for building relationships.

Don't make it hard for people to post a comment!

Passion, a plan and learning the blogging basics is just the start of the journey – then you need to come up with the ideas and then create the content that engages your audience. So how do you create content that people will read and keep them engaged and keep them coming back?

Step Four: Creating Content that Engages Your Audience

The foundation for any long lasting engagement on the web that will keep people coming back is content that educates, inspires and solves problems.

Essentially there are 3 steps you need to consider in the process:

1. Come up with ideas for content consistently.
2. Write headlines that will compel the reader to read.

3.   Structure the article so that the reader wants to keep on reading.

1. Ideas for Content

Coming up with ideas for content is a challenge for most bloggers. So here are 17 tips to help you assist you in coming up with ideas to create and develop content for your blog:

1. Read other top blogs and develop content on industry Trends – where is the industry going, what are the emerging hot segments?

2. Find out who your customers are and where they hang out, what they watch and what they read. Write and develop content that is in their language and publish it to the platforms that they frequent.

3. Write about customers' successes – if you publish a case study about a client's successful project, they will often let you include their name.

4. Publish content on what not to do; by highlighting where something hasn't worked. Naturally the names are anonymous.

5. Create a video blog post by interviewing a successful client – this can provide powerful evidence of authority and credibility for both you and the client.

6. Write articles for the different types of customers that are relevant for each of your vertical markets.

7. Brainstorm blog post topics with colleagues and management and create a list for future reference and planning.

8. Subscribe to the top industry blogs in your market for ideas – both company blogs and personal blogs.

9. Look through the latest news releases for ideas.

10. Invite others in your organization to write on topics in your industry or market that they are passionate about.

11. Interview successful people in your industry.

12. Turn your "how to" blog posts into short videos.

13. When you have a great idea, go straight to your "add new" button on your post section of your WordPress blog, write the headline, and save it as a

draft (or just write it down before you forget it – I use the notes feature on my iPhone to catch those moments of inspired thought).

14. Include a great iconic image at the start of your posts to catch the reader's eye.

15. Case Studies are always popular to write about and not just your own.

16. Upload your PowerPoint presentations to SlideShare, and embed them in your blog posts – this will allow people to view your presentations on the web, anytime and anywhere.

17. Run polls and surveys on your blog.

2. Headlines

You have the ideas for creating the content, but how do you get people to read it? The short answer: write a great headline!

So what are the important elements in creating and writing a "great headline" and why is it so important?

✓ Tests have shown that you can increase your conversion rate on a website or a link by 73% by the use of a compelling headline.

✓ On average, 8 out of 10 people will read headline copy, but only 2 out of 10 will go on to read the rest of the copy. This is the secret to the power of the headline, and why it so highly determines the effectiveness of the entire piece.

✓ Another test revealed that a good headline performed 259% better than the worst headline.

This means that up to nearly 3 times as many people would read your web page or view your video just through having spent some time ensuring that the headline is optimized.

So what are the basic requirements for writing that headline that will get people clicking and reading, viewing your content and copy?

6 Headline Formulas

One way to start is to use a formula, so here are 6 headline types and examples from Authority Blogger to get you started:

1. **Get What You Want** (In Health, Wealth, Relationships, Time and Lifestyle), for example: "The Secret To Getting More Money For Your Property!"

2. **Crystal Ball and History**, for example: "10 Predictions on the Future of Social Media"

3. **Problems and Fears**, for example "Get Rid of Your Debt Once and For All"

4. **Fact, Fiction, Truth and Lies**, for example: "Little Known Ways To Make Money On The Stock Exchange"

5. **How To, Tricks Of The Trade**, for example: "How To Plan The Ultimate Holiday"

6. **Best and Worst**, for example: "The 10 Worst Mistakes Made by Bloggers"

Another very effective headline strategy is to use is 'list' headlines and these are some examples that I have used:

- ✓ 50 Ways To Optimize Your Blog
- ✓ 30 Things You Should Not Share On Social Media
- ✓ The 7 Secrets to Ford's Social Media Marketing Success

You will notice that it is a 'list' format and includes numbers. A mega list headline is a large list such as "50 Ways to Optimize Your Blog" or "102 Proven Headline Formulas" and can be very effective. I have experimented with these types of headlines and they have produced some of my best blog traffic results.

Getting a handle on the basics of headline writing will make a big difference to your website and blog traffic especially when used in your online marketing

3. Structuring Your Content so it Begs to be Read

The reality of writing great content is that the headline is just the start! You want your visitor to stay and read the whole article rather than bounce out to another website in this era of 'click and go'.

We live in a world of ever decreasing attention and the art of keeping the reader engaged has now become an ongoing creative and scientific experiment of verbal and visual seduction.

The Age of Skimming

So writing that awesome headline has made the reader get started, but now you have to continue to entice, tease and intrigue the reader with the promise of more information, possible entertainment or a solution to the problem so that they will continue.

Skimming the article is the norm and with so much information competing for everyone's attention, constantly honing your writing skills is required to ensure that the information your post promised in the headline is readily available while as your readers eyes scan the page.

People are Seeking Answers

Readers are seeking solutions and answers to their problems. They are asking questions.

- ✓ Will this video embedded in the article deliver the information I crave?
- ✓ Will the embedded SlideShare presentation provide content that will help me with my next meeting or will impress my customer and my boss?
- ✓ Will the rest of the article enlighten me or bore me?

The headline is important on all of your content publishing, even on Facebook and especially on Twitter. Twitter has made the art of the headline more important than ever before because you only have 140 characters to tempt the potential reader to take action and click on the link that is embedded in your tweet.

The Headline is Only the Start of the Seduction

What you need to realize is that the headline is the start of the seduction – your reader needs to be continually visually and mentally arrested to keep them on your page.

Here are a variety of tips and tactics to continue to lure the reader deeper into your article beyond the headline so that they will not just click away to somewhere else.

The Intro

The introduction is next in importance after the headline. This is an art rather than a science but there are some good tactics to ensure that you don't lose them in the first sentence or paragraph.

Mastering the art of copywriting can be arduous, and the master copywriter Eugene Schwartz often spent days crafting the first 50 words of sales copy. As a blogger, you are in the business of selling your content, one post at a time, and you won't always have time to agonize over every introduction, so here are some suggestions to save you some time:

1. **Post a question.** Challenging the reader to think engages their mind and makes them want to find out the answer.

2. **Open with a quote.** This may inspire the reader to keep reading, in hopes of learning how the quote relates to your idea.

3. **Provide a powerful personal story.** A personal or powerful story can be the point of interest that keeps the reader and listener engaged, whether around the campfire, or within your articles.

4. **Quote an enticing fact or statistic.** If you are writing about Facebook it could be the fact that: "One in every eight minutes spent on the internet is on Facebook" to draw the reader in.

5. **Create context.** Lead into the main part of the article by creating the context for the rest of the story. Provide some background to the argument or solution that you are about to put forward. It could be the condensed history of the topic, or some facts and figures, or by stating of the problem that needs solving.

6. **Paint a mental picture.** It could be a sentence opening with phrases such as "imagine this..." or "do you remember when..."

7. **Analogies and other tricks.** You could try a phrase such as "A writer without a blog is like a salesman without a telephone" that captures the reader's attention.

8. **Use keywords.** This is one rule you should not ignore. What are the keywords people will be looking for when they arrive at your blog? Remember that you are writing for two categories of reader; your audience and the 1 million Google computer servers that are crawling and indexing your words, headlines and keywords. The challenge is to write naturally while remaining mindful of 'Lord Google'.

9. **Write subtitles.** Subtitles are mini headlines that entice your reader to continue reading; they are teasers that promise more intriguing and

inspiring content to follow. They also help visually break up the page – no one likes a straight block of text.

10. **Use images.** Images with screenshots including arrows and circles illustrating key points can be worth a thousand words, and make learning clear and easy to follow through on. Make the solution a "no-brainer".

11. **Consider a video.** Sometimes a short 2-minute video can offer the reader a quick way to understand a concept, idea or solution, in a way that 500 words cannot. This could be embedded half way through the story. Remember, you are writing for the web, and rich interactive media is both expected and demanded.

12. **Hyperlinks.** This is quite often overlooked and in a digital interconnected age the article that includes hyperlinks offers a depth and a breadth of information that makes the reader want to explore. Links or additional resources at the end of an article encourage the reader to read more of your valuable blog content. I also recommend setting up the links so that they open up in a new browser window, ensuring that the original page is still open, visible, and waiting on their return.

Format for Scanning and Skimming

A wall of straight text says one thing to a reader: "If you want the information… good luck in finding it, because it's buried here somewhere!"

So break it up into chunks that are easy to digest and don't create visual constipation.

This can be done in a variety of ways, such as:

- ✓ Italics
- ✓ Call out box or block quote
- ✓ Short paragraphs
- ✓ Bullet points
- ✓ A short numbered list

The Closing

Ending your piece is important and the main thing to remember is to close the loop by tying it back to the beginning. It could be a statement or a question.

And don't forget the call to action. This might be a phrase such as: "What is one thing that you can do today that you have learnt from this post?"

Step Five: How to Market to a Global Audience with Social Media

Ideas or content can lie undiscovered for years in the vain hope that someone will stumble across them with a Google search. The most vital step after content creation in the blogger's journey is to learn the art of marketing.

The new social web provides the all-important leverage of "world of mouth" to reach and engage with a global audience.

- ✓ Social media marketing has, at its core, a foundation of valuable, shareable content in all the various forms of rich media, whether it's text, video or images.
- ✓ People watch YouTube videos because they are entertaining, educational or funny.
- ✓ Viewers find your SlideShare account and take the time to view a PowerPoint presentation because the content is compelling.
- ✓ LinkedIn works well for personal branding because you are providing answers to your peers to questions in the Q&A section and providing updates that answers problems, informs and educates
- ✓ Twitter teases you to click on links that lead to engaging blog posts or news that is topical and timely.
- ✓ Facebook is where most of your audience is online so content needs to be posted and updated to the social giants' ecosystem.

Social media marketing is the most efficient way to spread your content and ideas to a global audience. The goal is to create a 'social media synergy' that totals a sum far greater than the individual parts. Most people think that Facebook "is" social media, but I would encourage you to use a multi-channel social media marketing approach.

194

The idea is to go beyond being just 'Facebook Centric' and provide substance, endurance and longevity to your on-line presence and digital assets. This will assist you in optimizing and integrating the various social media platforms.

Step Six: Maintaining the Momentum

Maintaining momentum in any sphere of your life is a challenge whether it's a business, a relationship or as a blogger, and there are no easy answers.

What I have discovered is that if the combination of innate ability and passion that you discovered and drove you from day one are true to your purpose then maintaining momentum will not be difficult.

What I have also found helpful are 3 key activities to maintain the energy and the forward motion:

- ✓ **Reading** – It doesn't matter if it is offline or online reading; it provides new ideas that will keep the inspiration flowing.
- ✓ **Sharing** – Talking to your tribe of likeminded people whether it is on Twitter or over a coffee or lunch will provide you with new insights and fuel to maintain the blogging momentum.
- ✓ **Disrupting** – Push yourself into new areas that will challenge you and will keep you learning and motivated.

Starting the journey is the easy part but true success is found in the persistence which will bring true self-discovery and a life that becomes a masterpiece.

Jeff Bullas (@JeffBullas) is an award winning blogger writing about social media marketing.
<u>Start of Audience Building</u>: *2009*
<u>Websites and Blogs</u>: *JeffBullas.com*
<u>Our Favorite Blog Post</u>: *How to Write a Mind Blowing Headline for Twitter So People Will Read Your Blog*

Jk Allen: Six Tips to Build an Engaged Audience from Scratch

Remember that every teacher was once a student.

One of the most rewarding aspects of blogging is having an engaged audience.

The challenge is building that audience from scratch. There's no right or wrong strategy to implement to obtain this goal, but there are some definite steps to consider along your journey.

In the time that I've spent blogging, I've developed a highly engaged audience.

I measure my audience's engagement by their interactions with my blog posts (valuable comments, emails, and social media sharing) and by their response to my calls to take action. I think it's important to note that "engagement" will look different depending on your platform and goals.

Below I've shared 6 tips that I would use if I had to build an engaged community from scratch. These tips are lessons that I picked up along the way in building my own engaged audience; whether I learned it the hard way, or took the advice from another. I hope they help with your journey.

1. Pick the Right Niche

This is one of the most critical areas in the early phase of developing an engaged audience. There are many branches that stem from the immense importance of this step. When deciding on the right niche, ask yourself the following questions:

- ✓ Can I write about this subject matter every day?
- ✓ Do I have enough interest to keep focused in this area?
- ✓ Do I have personal experiences within the niche that I'm willing to share with strangers?

Simply having an interest in a topic, in my opinion, isn't enough to consistently create the type of content that invokes interest and learning for others. Without these important keys, establishing an engaged audience will be nearly impossible to achieve.

Honestly assessing this key area means the difference between being able to provide meaningful content that offers value to your would-be audience and being stuck while trying to create your first bit of content.

2. Define Your Audience

When creating a product or service you have to determine who you're creating it *for*.

Your target audience doesn't just develop on its own; it's planned out well before launch. This is a crucial point because it will dictate the type of interaction you have with your audience.

Here's a quick example: the way you deliver your message to teenagers is very different from the way that you would deliver your message to a professional crowd.

Having a targeted audience within your scope doesn't mean that you'll be restricted to a single group; it means that you always have that group in mind and direct your content to their level and interests. If others decide to join ship, that's just icing on the cake.

3. Have a Humble Approach

Every teacher was once a student, and the best teachers remain students as forever.

Forgetting the importance of this dynamic can cause a rift between you and those that follow your work. Forgetting that you were once a student (or that you still are a student) can make you come across as arrogant. Writing with the assumption that everyone should know what you know, or believe what you believe is a recipe for destruction.

People, in general, don't like know-it-all's. It's okay to be imperfect and admit to being wrong. It's okay to share losses. Everyone experiences setbacks and challenges and if you can show that you're just as human as they are, they are more likely to find some attachment to what you have to share. If your content fails to display humility from time to time, the engagement of your audience won't reach its maximum level.

Being humble allows you to be relatable. Everyone experiences hardships, failing to share yours, will certainly create a rift over time.

4. Keep Focused

Bouncing from niche to niche and not having a narrow content focus creates brand confusion. If your readers are confused about your brand, they're engagement level will never peak.

If you fail to pick the right niche, you'll find yourself with a lack of creative juice to create content and feel the pressure to sway into other niches. I want to be clear that expanding your focus over time is fine and well, but initially, when building an engaged audience, it's important to have focus and a clear direction.

5. Write from Personal Experience

Writing from personal experience creates emotion and interest. There's nothing worse than reading dry content based solely on theory and non-practicality. Being able to create content from the direction of personal experience helps establish credibility, no matter the level of experience.

Incorporating this into your content makes for a personable experience for your audience, creating a landscape for higher engagement and interest. Failing to institute this can create a void due to a lack of relatability.

6. Request Interaction

If you want engagement, ask for engagement!

Many bloggers request dialog at the end of their posts. The purpose of this isn't just for the sake of it; it's to create interaction with the hopes of extending the overall value of the content.

In most instances, if content is layered with personal stories of experience, interaction will happen automatically. But asking the audience to participate helps widen the range of value because in the discussion will bring about different experiences and introduce new perspectives.

It takes time, but it's worth it!

An engaged audience is fun, rewarding and essentially what we all seek in our blogging and content creation efforts. An audience wants to engage; they want to interact, but we have to give them a reason to do so. We have to establish credibility and trust and relate with them on an emotional level. We have to be willing to share our personal stories; showing our depth of creativity and ability to provide value.

When I started blogging, it took time for my audience to grow to even a handful of readers.

But those readers carried a lot of power, because they engaged my content. My initial readers actually helped my readership multiply by way of sharing my content with the world through social media and linking back to my work, in their own work.

Today, my audience continues to grow, as does their engagement. I owe this to my application of the tips I've shared here. I hope they work the same magic for you.

JK Allen (@JKtheHustler) blogs about personal development, business and life over at the Hustler's Notebook – telling it like it is, and raising the bar for the rest of us.
Start of Audience Building: 2010
Websites and Blogs: HustlersNotebook.com
Our Favorite Blog Post: Who needs a MBA (or any Degree) When You Have Hustle?

Steve Scott: 12 Steps to Building an Engaged Audience

Working hard is not optional.

My name is Steve Scott and I am an Internet Marketer.

I know that those words, "Internet Marketer" carry a lot of negative weight.

It is easy to connect the words "Internet Marketer" solely with those guys who fill your email inbox with tons of spam.

Maybe you think about all the "Lose Weight with No Effort", "Push-button Success" and "Money without Work" ads that bombard you constantly while online. You know the stuff…

All of the promises that you can get something for nothing with zero effort required.

Yeah… I understand the negative reaction to the words, *"Internet Marketer"*. After all, how can you tell when an Internet Marker is lying? *His lips are moving!* (Ba dum bum! I'm here all night; please remember to tip your wait staff!)

The "Right" Way to Do Things

I do not believe in this type of marketing. You cannot get something from nothing. One way or another work is involved in everything worthwhile.

There is the vast majority of slick hucksters out there, and also some good marketers who are trying to make money by guiding you to good products. The difference is in effort and results.

The hucksters will tell you that can get great results from minimal effort. The real deal will show you the results, let you have an honest appraisal of the work and effort required, and trust the discerning customer to buy (or not).

What does this have to do with building an engaged audience?

You may be wondering, *"What this introduction has to do with building an engaged audience?"*

The answer is actually; quite a lot. It comes down to a word that some people simply hate to hear: effort.

You need to do the work.

You can't sign up for a few social networks and have people magically flock to your site because you are *that special.*

If you want to build an engaged audience, you will have to put in the effort and time. You will have to engage others yourself.

You will need to do the work!

What is this "work" I am talking about?

There is not one specific, "right" path to building an engaged audience. That's the genius of this book that you are reading. What works for me will not perfectly work for you. We are all individuals, and everyone has natural strengths and weaknesses.

But there are "general" ideas that will work for everyone to some degree. The important part is to really do the steps. Try out some of the ideas that I list, as well as those that others bring up. See what works for you! See what doesn't work. Cut back on the things that do not work and do more of the things that do work.

Simple.

The following is my 12 step program for building an engaged audience. It is by no means a complete list. These are the things *I would do* if starting out today.

The rating is not hierarchical. In other words I do not necessarily think #1 is more powerful than #10 or should always be done first.

Anyhow, enough jibber-jabber – let's get to the list!

ENGAGEMENT FROM SCRATCH!

1. Have a Game Plan

This can be as formal as a business plan with strict goals, or as informal as ideas scratched on the back of beer coasters. The important point is that you are not going to achieve success without an idea of what your goals and plans are.

Would you take a cross country trip without some sort of map or GPS? *Of course not!*

Set milestones, make goals and list the ways in which you are going to reach those goals. Be reasonable, but work hard to ensure you achieve all your goals.

2. Be a "Real" Person

It takes a lot of time to develop a real "voice" while writing. It is unlikely that you will start out with a natural writing voice. That is not a problem. Just make sure that you are being "yourself".

If you're new at something, be honest about it. Make that your selling point rather than a drawback. There is nothing worse than someone who claims to be an "expert" but clearly isn't.

Be yourself and keep it real!

3. Don't Think About Yourself

Getting people engaged is a funny thing. You can't think, *"I am going to spend 5 minutes a day on 'X's' site so he will become engaged."* Yes, you will need to allocate time every day. You will have to reach out to people. You will have to initiate and continue conversations.

But this scheduled time should be general. Find sites places and people that you like, and get into conversations. Some will pan out and some won't. An engaged audience consists of your friends, and you don't gain friends with *"I did X,Y,Z."* You gain friends by having people you enjoy being around and talking too. Your engaged audience will be people *that you want* to spend time talking with!

4. Get Out There and Find Others

Your engaged audience will consist of people with similar interests to you. The one great thing about the internet is that it brings people together. No matter how specific or strange your viewpoints, are there are likely thousands of people who will rabidly agree with you.

Get out there and find them:

✓ Do searches for blogs with keywords.

✓ Read some articles.

✓ When you find sites you like; comment on them.

✓ Add the sites to some sort of database (I use Excel).

One random comment will not create a lifelong friend, but if you leave enough intelligent comments, you can be sure to attract notice.

5. Be Everywhere

A lot of audience-building success is about reaching critical mass. Having guest posts on lots of sites will not only find you a new audience, but will also create a buzz and reminds people who have visited you before to drop in again.

This is a step that has direct bearing on how much effort you are willing to put in.

An occasional guest post here-and-there should be a bare minimum. But you can really bombard your niche with guest posts if you are willing to put in the effort.

6. Always Reply

There is some debate on how and to what depth someone should reply to comments.

Let me clear this up quickly: the debate is for people who *have* engaged audiences.

If you *want* an engaged audience, the only way you are going to get one is to engage them. That means that if someone takes the time to leave a thoughtful comment, you damn well better take the time to at least acknowledge it!

No debate: Always try to reply all comments until you reach the point where you have so many that it becomes impractical to do so. That is what we call a *good problem*.

7. Be Likeable

It may seem funny that we have gone so far in this list without yet mentioning content.

Good content is a must, no doubt about it.

But people will really become engaged with *you*, not just your content.

You want to be liked, but step #2 still applies (be the "real" you).

If you are a curmudgeon; be a curmudgeon. Just be a likeable curmudgeon. How you do this is all about personal style. You can be funny. You can be honest. You can be personal. You can be knowledgeable. Chances are you will be a few of these.

8. Work on Content

Okay, it is not all about the *'tude* – you definitely need some substance to your scribblings.

You *do* have things that will interest people; whether it is from a beginner's viewpoint or an expert's vantage. You can spice up your content by packaging it in different ways.

Here are a few of the "types" of articles that people respond to:
- ✓ Ask Questions
- ✓ Lists
- ✓ Funny
- ✓ Actionable
- ✓ Heartfelt

These all fall under the category of link-bait.

These are the types of articles that people naturally want to comment, tweet and share with others. Every article will not be link-bait, but you should try to do each type every so often.

9. Social Media: Be a Master; not a "Jack of all Trades"

One of the mistakes that I made early on was trying to have a presence on too many social media networks. This just ensures that none of the social networks will work for you.

It is far better to spend your time creating a strong presence on one social network. Really connecting with people, and becoming a thought leader rather than just another person blasting out personal links.

Which brings us to…

10. Be a Content Curator

Part of the reason you may invest time and energy in social networks is to get your message out there. But if that is *all* you do, your connection with other people will be minimal. It is far better to be a content curator.

Tweet and link others people's quality work. Use social media as a vehicle to both praise and promote others as well as yourself. Become a thought leader on your topic.

11. Find a Tribe/Community

This is a step that I am admittedly not an expert in, but there are many outstanding tribes, communities, and forums out there. These are groups of people that try to help each other get noticed and promoted.

This can be on a formal or informal basis; but having a group of people "in your corner" who can act as sounding boards, sanity checks and general help in sending out your message can only be a positive thing.

12. Gain Feedback and Adjust Your Plans Accordingly

Every good plan works in a loop. Over time you *must* get feedback on what works for you and what doesn't.

Measure your results.

Results will not appear overnight, so do not micro-manage those results; just be sure that over a long enough time frame, you measure what works and what doesn't.

ENGAGEMENT FROM SCRATCH!

You will need to do this for yourself. Expert A may claim that Twitter is a complete waste of time while Expert B will say that it is the only way to really create a really engaged audience. To see if ANY step or idea works you need to give it real try and see if it *works for YOU*.

If something does not work for you over a long time frame you need to try a different approach and then begin to measure those results. This will lead you right back to step 1: creating a new plan.

After that it is just a matter of constant refining as you continue to grow and engage your audience.

Good Luck!

Steve Scott (@stevescott1) is a blogger and business consultant who teaches people how to live the internet lifestyle.
Start of Audience Building: 2005
Blog and Websites: SteveScottSite.com
Our Favorite Blog Post: Developing the 30 Day Success Habit

Tyler Tervooren: The Fundamentals are Timeless

Be a leader, show humility, be consistent, move forward.

How do you build an audience online? Or offline? Or anywhere else in the infinite universe? That's the $64,000 question, isn't it?

Truth is, it isn't that hard.

Of course, it isn't a walk in the park either. Like many things in life, it's simple, but not always so easy. The basic principles of community building have been the same since the dawn of man, and anyone can learn them. But in today's world, we're bombarded with "shiny objects" – new tools and tidbits of advice to help us build our audiences faster or better or smarter or cheaper.

This is the dilemma of technology. New tools are good. Improvement is good. But, just like a carpenter with a $20,000 jig saw, until you have a solid foundation to build on – an understanding about why the tool exists and how to use it – **you're more likely to lose a finger than to gain an exquisite piece of furniture**.

But enough about missing digits. I have a feeling that you already know this to be true. You know that rallying the troops around your important cause is hard work that takes a deep understanding of people and why they do the things they do.

What you're looking for is a better understanding of these fundamentals. You want to know how to recognize them and how you can use them to build interest and loyalty for your most important work. So that's what we're going to focus on here. We'll leave the "10 quick tips" and "instant success" pieces to the hucksters.

Before we begin, though, a very important question: "Why me? What do I know?" It's a fair question, and the answer is "not that much."

It's true. I don't know a whole lot about this. I don't have decades of research under my belt or a giant repository of knowledge in my brain for random access. All

I have is a lot of experience from the school of hard knocks – years of trial and error that have boiled down to a few key points that I keep in mind whenever I want people to pay attention to something.

I don't have a lot, but what I've got seems to work very well. Let me illustrate with a story.

Growing up in a small, conservative town, I spent most of my life believing that the safest path through life – get a steady job, find a nice girl, buy a reliable car, have a few kids and wait for retirement – was the right one for me. Or at least, it seemed like that was the "right answer", because that's what everyone else I knew was doing. So that's what I did (minus the kids). And I was miserable. Of course, I didn't know why I was miserable; I was doing everything right!

When I eventually got fired from my job, I knew I had to try something different, but I wasn't sure what. So, I spent some time thinking about what had made me the happiest in the past, and when I realized that my greatest moments all happened when I was taking a risk, I knew I had to pursue it further. I made a list of all kinds of crazy risks I wanted to take in my life and started thinking about how to actually do them.

I quickly realized that making a big change is a risk in and of itself, and it was… *scary*. But I thought it was worthwhile enough – and interesting enough – that perhaps a few other people would be interested in joining me for the journey. So I built a website to act as my own support group.

Three months later there were 2,000 people along for the ride, and the site's been growing steadily ever since. And a funny thing happened very early on that helped the audience grow exponentially – I started to realize how interesting the people were that came to read my story. There were people taking fun, meaningful, and adventurous risks in their own lives, and I was only one of many.

I started for selfish reasons, but the site really exploded **when I realized the potential of the people around me**. And that's what makes the difference between a website and a community. It's the defining line between an "audience" and a "movement". Anyone can build a website, but it takes a special vision to create a thriving community.

Beyond just a special vision, though, I learned four other very important lessons about building a community. Since that's what you're trying to do, I want to share them with you:

Lesson #1: A Community Requires Leadership

Things started to change for me once I decided to take real ownership of my ideas. When I quit simply talking about my big plans and started doing them, many more people began to pay attention. And not only did they start to pay attention, but they started to report back with their own ideas and taking on their own challenges.

To be an effective leader, you must inspire.

And to inspire, you must not only deliver your message through words, but through actions. They say that a good boss never asks her employees to do something she isn't willing to do herself. If you want to build a community for your important cause, you have to think of yourself as a "good boss."

Live your message.

Lesson #2: A Community Requires Humility

To build and lead any community to do great things, you have to accept that you don't have all the answers. This can be intimidating when you feel like you're responsible to get things right all the time, but a great community is built on great humility and the understanding that the best answer often comes from the community itself.

Making the final decision is your responsibility – you're the leader, after all – but you don't have to come up with all the solutions. Humble yourself and ask your community what it wants. Whether it's through email, surveys, blog comments, or some other method, reach out and ask your people what they want.

And don't be afraid to learn from others who've gone before you. You can't copy success, but you can certainly learn from it. Why else would you be reading this book right now?

And don't just learn. Learn, and then act. This sequence can also be reversed. It's the only way to progress.

Lesson #3: A Community Requires Consistency

It's difficult for people to invest themselves in something if they're uncertain that it will be around for long. Something that's temporary or fragile is less appealing than something that's permanent and solid.

When you ask someone to become a part of your community – to join your audience – you might not realize that you're asking them to trade a significant piece of their life. Time, attention, and commitment are things of which we all have a limited amount to give. Think about the audiences that you've become a part of over time. What drew you to them? Did you invest yourself in something that looked like it might disappear the next day?

Give people a reason to believe that you're here for the long haul, and you'll have a much easier time convincing them to stick around. Longevity is a powerful motivator.

Lesson #4: A Community Requires Forward Motion

Perhaps the very most important aspect of any successful community is the perception that it's going somewhere. Again, think about the communities you give your time to. Did you invest yourself in them hoping that you'd stay the same as you were before? Or did you join them because you saw a powerful force at work that was helping people propel themselves forward, and you wanted to be a part of it?

Do you have a mission statement that's easy to understand and explains exactly what I can expect to gain by joining your community? Stagnation is as good as death when it comes to organizing a group. People don't want to just be led; they want to be led *somewhere*.

These four rules are, without a doubt, the most important things I've ever learned about building a community. In the face of ever changing technology, tips, and tricks, these four pillars seem to remain whether you're building a township in ancient times, a union of organized laborers in the heart of the industrial revolution, or a present-day web community of like-minded people. And as long as it's humans we're organizing, these rules will exist for whatever trend the future ushers in next.

While they're easy to understand, they're not always so simple to implement. While building my own community, I made many mistakes along the way.

- ✓ I made promises that I couldn't keep and lost the trust of my members.
- ✓ I built up momentum and then let it fade, having to build it all over again.
- ✓ I found strategies that worked and then abandoned them when I got bored.
- ✓ I tried to copy the success of others.
- ✓ I geeked out on things that didn't matter and half-assed the things that did.
- ✓ I compared myself to others and lost motivation when I didn't measure up.

I've made so many mistakes that it's sometimes embarrassing to admit. Yet, the community I started continues to grow. I believe the reason for this is because I always tried to maintain my focus on those four very important rules:

1. Be a leader
2. Show humility
3. Be consistent
4. Move forward

When you do that, I think you naturally tend to build something much bigger than yourself, and that's what a community, in its truest form, is all about. You can make mistakes, and life still goes on – because the community no longer depends entirely on you to get everything right.

Maybe that should be rule number five: Never be afraid to screw everything up.

Happy community building!

Tyler Tervooren (@TylerTervooren) promotes "better living through uncertainty" and about living your best, most adventurous life.
Start of Audience Building: 2010
Blogs and Websites: AdvancedRiskology.com, TylerTervooren.com
Our Favorite Blog Post: The Simple Secrets of a $100 Business

Conclusion

There you have it – 30 perspectives on how to build an engaged audience from scratch (31 if you count mine). Some of the contributors, like Guy Kawasaki and Brian Clark, have audiences that number in the millions. Others, like Stuart Mills and Jk Allen, are just getting started, and have audiences that 'only' number in the thousands. What is constant is that every single contributor to this book has the ear of at least several thousand people, at least a portion of which looks to them for advice, guidance, and inspiration.

I didn't know what to expect when I started creating this book. I wanted it to be general enough to be broadly applicable, but tactical enough to be practical; theoretical enough to give readers new insight and understanding, but down-to-earth enough for them to be able to take what they read and make things happen.

If this sounds like a set of crazy contradictions, that's because it is, and in my attempts to meet all of these requirements, I probably gave the book's contributors an impossible set of instructions. Which is why it's such a good thing that they set my instructions aside, dug deep, and shared their own perspective and story instead.

You see, when I set out to write this book, I thought I knew how to build an audience. I knew what ingredients were needed, and I knew what recipe to follow to turn those ingredients into an engaged community. I was just going to get a bunch of smart people to each tell the part of the story that they knew best.

Only it turns out that I was wrong. A lot of what the contributors submitted was well thought-out, brilliant, eminently useful… and new to me. Do I agree with all of it? No, I don't. Hell, some of the ideas in this book contradict other ideas in this book – and that's okay, because there are many paths up the mountain, and looking for the 'one true path' is probably the biggest mistake that you can make (as Stuart Mills reminded us in his chapter of the book).

The bottom line is that whether I agree or not, this stuff works – every single person who contributed to this book has followed their own advice to build a thriving audience. Will it work for me? Will it work for you? Maybe not. We all have to find our own path up that mountain. But we learn from the examples, insights and experiences of all of the contributors to this book, are we ready to forge our own path up that mountain?

You bet we are!

Postscript: The Most Important Thing

The most important thing was perfectly captured by one of the people who had a look at a pre-release copy of the book. She wrote to me that:

> *"The common denominator was the "I care about my readers" element, the desire to "build a community through relationships." This book is about MORE than just engaging, it is about caring, connecting & building. Caring about the readers, connecting those relationships and building that community."*

I couldn't have put it better myself. So take these lessons to heart as you go forth and build your audience:

Care about your readers.

Connect with them.

And build your community.

Good luck!

Thank You

To say that writing a book is a team effort would be the understatement of the year, and that is truer of this book than most others. There's a long list of people who deserve thanks, starting with all thirty of my co-authors, who generously invested their time and insight into this project.

Just as deserving of thanks is my talented and dedicated assistant, Megan Dougherty. She is the only person who may have spent more hours working on this book than I did, and without her tireless research and diligent editing, I definitely wouldn't have been able to find the time to see this project to completion.

I would also like to thank Remi Delon at WebFaction, and Kara Udziela and Par Gandhi at Photos.com for their generous financial support of this project, and Dan Delany at the Network for Teaching Entrepreneurship for allowing me to make a contribution to their very deserving organization.

Also deserving of recognition are the many, many wonderful people throughout my life who have very kindly given me their guidance and advice, and who took a chance on me when they didn't have to. They are too numerous to thank, and there is nothing they need from me, but I hope that they will take some small pleasure in knowing that when I do the same for others, it is by virtue of their examples.

Much of this book was written and compiled while my wife and I planned our wedding. Writing a book is a massive undertaking, and so is planning a wedding – doing them together is borderline crazy, and the only reason I was able to pull it off was because of the incredible support of the people closest to us, particularly my brothers Yoni and Ari Iny, my sister-in-law Sheetal Pathak, my uncle Ronnie Iny, and my aunt Vera Iny.

ENGAGEMENT FROM SCRATCH!

No acknowledgements section could ever be complete without my parents, Ruthy Daniel and Mayer Iny, who have taught me a lot of the important things that I know, and given me the confidence and encouragement to learn the rest.

And last, but certainly not least, my deepest thanks go out to my wonderful wife, Bhoomi Pathak. She was my companion from this book's inception and straight through to its publication, and my sounding board at every step along the way. She raised her glass to celebrate every single victory ("Brian Clark agreed to participate!", "I got our first sponsor!", "The trailer is looking great!", and dozens of others), and was my support and strength on all the days that there weren't any victories to report. Sweetie, I love you with all my heart, and thank you so, so much, for everything.

DANNY INY
MONTREAL, CANADA

Support the Teaching of Entrepreneurship

Too many young people today drop out of school and struggle to break the cycle of poverty.

Since 1987, the Network for Teaching Entrepreneurship (NFTE) has been inspiring young people to pursue educational opportunities, start their own businesses, and succeed in life.

By providing entrepreneurship education programs relevant to the real world, NFTE empowers students to own their educations in and out of the classroom and to find their own path to success.

Hundreds of thousands of students have discovered opportunity all around them through entrepreneurship via thousands of certified educators worldwide. The NFTE supports active programs in 21 states and 10 other countries through our network of program offices and licensed partners. Entrepreneurs are a powerful driver of economic growth and NFTE sows the seeds of innovation in students worldwide.

Do your part to help the cause, and make somebody's life a little better, and more filled with opportunity. You can buy a copy of this book, and 50% of profits from book sales will be donated to the NFTE. Or you can make a donation directly – visit www.NFTE.com for details.

ENGAGEMENT FROM SCRATCH!

Sponsors and Special Offers

This book was made possible by the generous support of our sponsors, who are introduced to you in the following pages.

We were careful only to associate with brands that are in the business of creating value for people who are just setting out to build an audience, and we insisted that our sponsors create a very special offer for our readers.

So please take a moment to learn about our sponsors, and what they can do for you.

WebFaction: Smarter Web Hosting

WebFaction has been providing web hosting since 2003 to thousands of companies and individuals all over the world. The  company is privately owned, has been profitable since day 1 and uses some of the best datacenters in the world.

We are known for our outstanding customer service, our support for all the latest software and our undercrowded servers leading to faster websites.

We provide one-click installers for dozens of popular apps including WordPress, Drupal, Django, Rails and more.

Our servers also come with all the tools needed to build your own apps, making us an ideal choice for start-ups whether your app is written in PHP, Python, Ruby or others.

ENGAGEMENT FROM SCRATCH!

Our setup also includes the ability to scale to multiple instances within minutes so you can cope with traffic if your app gets popular.

Visit www.WebFaction.com for details, or to get started with your own professional hosting package today.

SPECIAL OFFER FOR READERS: Save $50 when you sign up by using the promotional code "ENGAGEMENT".

Photos.com: Stock photos for less. A lot less.

Photos.com is a leading source of both professionally shot and user-generated content. We offer over 2.5 million royalty-free stock photos and illustrations with releases—available as single images, image packs or subscriptions, so you can save based on your project needs. Customers use our compelling, high quality images and illustrations to help improve their advertising, presentations, websites, blogs, sales brochures, direct mail, email and more.

They're a division of Getty Images – a leading creator and distributor of still imagery, editorial imagery, footage and music in the world.

Photos.com has single images starting at $1.99, image packs that start as low as $0.90 image, and subscriptions starting as low as $0.19 an image.

Visit www.Photos.com for details, or to get started with your own professional-quality images and illustrations.

SPECIAL OFFER FOR READERS: Save 10% on your purchases by using the promotional code "B4XPC46N" when you checkout.

Firepole Marketing: We Turn Non-Marketers into Expert Marketers

If you want to make more money, we can help.

If you're getting started in business, we can help.

Here's the deal:

If you want to grow your business and make more money, then there are some things that you need to understand:

Who your customer really is…

…why your stuff is really valuable to them

…and how to communicate that value in a way that makes them want to buy from you.

There's a word for all that, and that word is MARKETING! That's exactly what we teach: MARKETING.

We turn non-marketers into expert marketers. We do it with our training program, we do it with our coaching clients, and we do it with our $197 FREE video training on how to Get More Cash Out of Any Business, Website or Blog… In Under 30 Days, Without Spending Money, Working More Hours, or Hiring Staff. Get it here:

bit.ly/GetMoreCash

About Danny Iny

Danny Iny has been an entrepreneur for longer than his entire adult life. He quit school when he was fifteen to start his first business, and has been doing it ever since.

Along the way he ran the Montreal Marathon, got an MBA, and married the most wonderful woman in the world. He's also worked with companies of all sizes, from the very huge (Nokia, Google) to small businesses and entrepreneurs who are just getting started.

These days, he is a prolific blogger and teacher in the Firepole Marketing training program, and enjoys working one-on-one with client businesses to improve their marketing and make more money.

He's also the author of a book about effective communication in writing, university guest lecturer, and the CEO of a start-up company called Motiv808.

In addition to all of the above, Danny is a super-friendly guy who makes a point of responding to every email and message – so go ahead and follow him on Twitter @DannyIny, or just send him an email (to danny@FirepoleMarketing.com), and say hello!

Do You Need Help Building Your Own Engaged Audience?

This book contains the most important lessons learned by some of the world's most successful audience- and community-builders about how they built an engaged and loyal audience, and how they would do it all again.

To help you put their advice into practice, we've created a whole goodie bag of extra stuff for you:

- ✓ Detailed infographics clearly laying out the entire process taught in the book
- ✓ Worksheets to help you do everything that is discussed in the book, and do it well
- ✓ Templates that you can use to approach bloggers and build relationships
- ✓ Access to exclusive teleseminars, webinars, and coaching calls
- ✓ And a whole bunch of other cool stuff…

Does that sound awesome or what? Go get it now:

bit.ly/efs-bonus

12263337R00137